Lessons Learned

the Hard Way

Dr. Victor Couzens

Lessons Learned the Hard Way
Copyright © 2020 by Dr.Victor Couzens

ISBN 978-1-63684376-6

Dr. Victor Couzens

Table of Contents

Acknowledgments

To the men who rode the storm out with me publicly, fearlessly and unapologetically through the season that birthed this book;

L Lawrence Brandon

Bill Curtis

Michael Dickerson

John Guns

Brehon Hall

Jawane Hilton

Brian Hodges

Darnell Lee

Carlos Malone

Aaron Marble

Willie McCalla

Devin Owens

James Paulk

Earnest Pugh

Al Reese

Quentin Respress *Covenant

Xavier Thompson *Broski

Thank you!

To Bishop Corletta J. Vaughn, the epitome of spiritual parenting, covering, wisdom, love, and fidelity. Thank you for challenging me to show up for me.

To the people of Inspirational Bible Church; Your prayers, support, patience, and encouragement have been my lifeline. I love you all.

Last but not least, my wife, Abigail. You prayed when I could not, and you stood when the chips were down. Thank you. I love you.

Foreword as written by
Apostle Carlos L. Malone, Sr.

Every human vessel, saved and unsaved, will face various episodes of tests, temptations, and trials. The only avoidable element in this is to try and keep these episodes away from public scrutiny due to the unreliable support of friends and reliable criticism and judgment that incubates within the social media sector. Not only that, but the church has, on so many occasions, found itself on the wrong side of grace and restoration and continues to hibernate itself in denial on that subject. Love is the foundation of our Christian heritage, but at times it's hard to notice based upon how we adjudicate falsely the biblical teachings of Jesus Christ and men such as the Apostle Paul. It is upon this foundation of both truth and human reality that I pen this commendation and endorsement of not just this book but its author Dr. Victor Couzens.

It is so easy for us to highlight our stars that bling in success through the public spotlight, but not many of us want our scars of failure and human weakness to be revealed, exposed, or discovered. But in this scenario, Dr. Couzens doesn't present to us hyperbole laced theories or fantasy episodes of the mind. Still, he transparently talks to us from the place of his own experiences. He did not intentionally drive himself to this place as if it was a part of his personally planned schedule. Not so, this is God using this man of God's publicly exposed failures as an instrument for his deliverance, development, and discipline. See, the enemy will use people to expose us, but God will use that exposure of embarrassment to execute his justice, mercy, and grace. You see, public exposure in the faith community is the last of 3 steps when dealing with a fallen believer, and even then, that exposure should be limited to that local assembly.

In this book, Lessons Learned the Hard Way, Dr. Couzens takes us on a real-life journey as well as a practical and biblical tour into the challenge of taking on personal responsibility, accountability, and remorse. The personal principles that he openly shares are given to correct those erroneous perversions and proclivities that will rule and ruin our lives if left undisciplined. By the right of his spiritual heritage, he clings to the cross of Jesus Christ for his redemption and restoration. Still, by right of refusal and personal responsibility, he doesn't use this grace as a crutch and excuse for his failures in these matters. I encourage you to read this book with an open mind and heart and learn from this man of God those truths and experiences that can help you face your own personal issues. As he states so

Dr. Victor Couzens

accurately, read this book as though you are reflecting in a mirror, not looking through a window.

Congratulations, My Lil Brother. I am so honored to stand and watch and to support and walk with you as you allow God to navigate you into your next dimension of his purpose for your life. Now that you have shared your truth keep looking and living beyond the negative critique of criticism and the shameful shadow of having your life laid out naked for the world to judge. Remember, according to accurate biblical accuracy, you did not fall from grace, you fell into grace, and for those who do not understand that, they should read Galatians chapter 5. God Bless You!!

Apostle Carlos L. Malone, Sr.

Preface

A Jewish King once said, "It was good for me that I was afflicted that I might learn thy statutes."

Learning comes in many different ways. Sometimes learning takes place in a room filled with desks and chairs. At other times learning takes place via online webinars and tutorials. But learning also takes place by living through specific experiences. I once heard someone state, "experience is the best teacher." If that is true, we should always lean into our experiences to evaluate what they can teach us.

Though sometimes uncomfortable, unwarranted, and even unfair, some experiences can teach, reinforce, and expose us to truths that we otherwise would not learn.

Uncomfortable experiences and adversity test the limits of our emotional, social, spiritual, and even relational capacity. Revealing our vulnerabilities and blind spots while at the same time serving as a precipice to rebuild and reinvent our lives.

Imagine a beautiful vase. It's splendid in its design and ornate in its shape. Now, let's say that beautiful vase is knocked over and shatters into several pieces. There are three options. One is to throw the broken pieces away. The second is to try and put the vase back together so that it will at least resemble what it once was, even though it may never hold water the way it previously did and may be a little unstable. The third and often the best option is to take the pieces and make something new, different, and perhaps even better.

Like many people, my life has had its ups and downs, twists, and turns. I have lost relationships, been shunned, kicked out of organizations, denied opportunities, misunderstood, and made unhealthy decisions. Unlike most people, some of my life experiences have not been contained or handled privately. Yet, there are incredible positive learning opportunities in each of the things mentioned above.

Dealing with personal setbacks and navigating public shame can be difficult. If you speak up, then you are perceived as being defensive and arrogant. If you are silent, then well, it's assumed that what is being said must be true. As a result, some people will stand with you privately but distance themselves from you publicly because they can't afford to have their brand compromised or they have things in their lives they don't want to resurface. Or they just don't have the grace or patience to go through it with you.

However, some people will not only stand with you; they will even hold your arms up and speak words of encouragement, accountability, and affirmation over you.

Dr. Victor Couzens

At the risk of being misunderstood and vexing some people, I decided to write this book anyway. This book needed to be written. Not as a public rebuttal, clap back, or defense but as a way to hopefully help and heal people who can identify with hardship.

It has been said that we are the sum total of our experiences and that a wise man learns not only from his mistakes but also from others' mistakes. So, I want to share with you what I have learned about personal setbacks, sometimes the hard way, with the hope that it will inspire you, grow you, and give you a greater sense of empowerment. My mission is to challenge and motivate you to keep living forward, no matter what happens in your life.

The purpose of this book is not to offer a philosophical approach to facing and overcoming challenges; it is to provide practical ways to establish guardrails for your life and identify blind spots (because all of us have them). I want to give you useful strategies to confront internal emotional bullies and work through constraining internal mire. While simultaneously owning the things that we do to create unnecessary hardship in our lives.

As you read, you will have the opportunity to gain insight from scripture, illustrations, real-life situations, and my personal experiences on how to get the most out of unpleasant life experiences, face strongholds, and endure hard-fought battles.

I hope you will read this, not in anticipation of getting my side of the story on any of the public scandal. My side of the story is not nearly as important as the outcomes realized by having walked through the fire of public scandal. Endured the pain of relational misfortune and undergone the heartache of betrayal.

Whatever you face in life can help you to grow, overcome, learn, and win.

I hope that by sharing these "Lessons Learned the Hard Way" and how I learned them, you will be refined and renewed in your thinking about what it takes to overcome.

Again, the content herein is not a mere hypothesis or conjecture, but it is wisdom birthed out of personal experience. My original audience for this book was vast and varied. Still, alas, I realize that this book appeals directly and exclusively to those interested in living a life that achieves high impact optimizes emotional currency, strives in perpetual growth, and maximizes spiritual maturity.

Should you choose to accept it, your mission is to read this book as though you are looking into a mirror as opposed to gazing through a glass window.

Dr. Victor Couzens

Chapter Zero: To My Brothers

As men. We all need a baseline. A starting point. A ground zero. One of the definitions of ground zero is; A starting point or base for some activity. Therefore, instead of just jumping into the heart of the matter and getting into the thick of things. I'd like to offer some thoughts and observations on being a man. More particularly, the journey and sometimes all-out war involved in truly becoming a man.

I don't offer these observations as one who has mastered them. But, as a brother in the trenches still trying to work through some of these things.

I have learned that being a man is a full-time job and insanely hard work. Not to say the same isn't true about being a woman.

One of the unique nuances about being a man is that there's no standard rite of passage or entryway into manhood in Western Civilization. Thus, many males struggle with a sense of insignificance and insecurity while stumbling and fumbling into being a grown man. Searching aimlessly to identify the unarticulated, unspoken, and indiscernible line of accessing manhood.

Like many males, I, too, have struggled with this.

A few years ago, I had the privilege of spending five days in Kenya, Africa, with the Maasai tribe. Particularly in the Suswa village. Until recent times becoming a man in the Maasai tradition and achieving warrior status required killing a lion. That was the right of passage. That was the ground zero. Wanna be a man? Kill a lion.

The Maasai people believed killing a lion demonstrated bravery and personal achievement.

Conceivably in Kenya, you could be a 30-year-old male and not be a man because you hadn't killed a lion. Not that I'm suggesting lion killing should be a thing. But there was a baseline. Something that formally acknowledged a man's ascent into manhood.

Boys would be trained and schooled on where to look for the Lions. What weapons to use and what to do with the lion after the kill.

When the newly minted warriors would return, a full week of celebration would take place. The women would gather around and embrace and congratulate the boy now turned man. They would receive *Imporro*, a double-sided beaded shoulder strap only reserved for a victor.

In American culture, with all of our advantages and advances. We do not have a ground zero for becoming a man. Is it biological, automatically occurring when a male reaches the age of 18 or 21? Is it economical and occurs when a male gets his first job and paycheck? Is it social and occurs after your first drink? Is it sexual and happens after your first sexual experience? Is it religious and occurs after baptism or when a male no longer has to attend children's church? When the heck is it? Do we know? Is it published anywhere?

Even the Western church of which I am part of with all of its liturgy, conferences, and the sort has no progressive corporate approach to what makes a man a man.

When I was a kid, I spent a lot of time watching the discovery channel with my grandfather. They used to run these shows about Jacques Cousteau. Among the many things he was famous and renowned for. He was a French explorer who avidly studied the sea.

Cousteau didn't investigate the sea for the sake of novelty. He was a shipwreck expert. He would scour the ocean floor in search of treasure that had been sunken and lost. In other words, he was on a mission to find sunken treasure. His quest was worthy of pirates of old.

And his quest, along with the Maasai people, also teach us a lot about a male becoming a man.

One of Jacques's most celebrated expeditions was to the Silver Bank, a coral reef in the Caribbean. There he unearthed the remnants of a shipwreck that happened centuries earlier and lay on the ocean floor covered by the different forms of life in the tropical waters. Undeterred and with a keen eye, Cousteau was able to recognize treasure even surrounded by debris, trash, and other particles.

I believe there is a parable included in that last sentence. Part of coming into manhood is beginning to see things, not as they appear to be but for what they really are. There's an acute adjustment to the sight of a man. Men see the world and themselves differently than just males do.

Titles don't make you a man. No more than owning a hammer makes you a carpenter, or making a baby makes you a father. I have learned that being a man is learned behavior.

Being a man involves a perpetual state of growing, evolving, and becoming.

The voyage of Cousteau and the former rite of passage of the Maasai teaches us another valuable truth about being a man.

Men are mission-driven. The seas of life will get rough sometimes. The ship might even take on water, and sometimes life will seem like a jungle, and you will wonder how you keep from going under, but men, men are driven by the mission. A man without a sense of mission is in a dangerous and vulnerable predicament.

He who has a why to live can bear
almost any how - Nietzsche

Mission anchors a man's principles. Mission makes decisions easier to make. Mission helps a man to eliminate impediments. Mission sets our priorities in order. Mission induces the wisdom required to be a prudent decision-maker. Mission gives a man the boldness and the permission needed to go against the tide when necessary. Be a pioneer. Get in good trouble, as the late John Lewis would say. This is the power of a brother who has a clear mission

It's when that mental shift occurs, and we lock in on a mission that glorifies God. Improves the lives of others and is worthy of imitation that we are excelling in manhood. All three tenants should be present.

There is a treasure in every man. It doesn't matter where you came from. It matters what you're made of. It takes work to get to the treasure sometimes, and sometimes it takes time to value your treasure. But as men, we cannot claim manhood or expect the respect and honor that comes with being a man if we are not mindful of our treasure. Let's not lean on our vocational or career titles while failing to cultivate our treasure.

Jacques Cousteau would literally find treasure in the moss and sometimes trash of tropical waters. Let's not find our inner treasure and yet fetish the garbage or debris that surrounds it.

How we see things is an indication of manhood. The mental shift towards mission is an indication of manhood. Respect for your treasure is a marker of manhood.

We might not be sea explorers like Cousteau but, every man is on a journey, a mission. It's a spiritual journey. Even if you're not a religious man or a man who is part of the Christian community. Regardless as to rather or not you are even a praying man. My brothers, we are each on a spiritual journey. Each man must accept responsibility for his journey.

God created men to establish and create order in the earth according to Genesis 2:15

God created us to cultivate what's under our influence according to the same text.

The bend towards manhood includes a man becoming more and more God-conscious.

God conscience is not the keeping of laws. It is growing in and learning to love. Loving yourself, loving your community, and loving your God.

What does a man on a spiritual journey of love look like?

It starts in the heart. We are shifting towards manhood when we begin to pursue a covenant with God. Covenant with God transforms a man, making him better, more responsible, and more fruitful.

Covenant with God compels a man to love himself and love his community enough to set his heart on a life of love and submission to God.

As men, we are sometimes good at playing to the crowd and telling people what they want to hear—and showing people what they want to see. But that's not manhood; that's manipulation.

Our spiritual journey demands that integrity be a real aim and mission for us. Integrity is by no means perfection. Integrity is serving others (Mark 10:45). It's is accepting responsibility for our actions and decisions (1 Timothy 4:12). It is being bold in the face of injustice (Micah 6:8). Integrity is honoring our bodies as the temple of God (1 Corinthians 6:19-20). It is being patient and kind and disciplined (Galatians 5:22-23). It is being honest and humble about where your gifts and talent and life and blessings come from (Philippians 2:3). It is being who God made you and not trying to be someone or something that you're not (1 Corinthians 15:10). It is repenting when you come up short (1 John 1:9), and it is desiring to please the Lord (2 Corinthians 5:9).

The good news is no brother has to be a skilled sailor, an African warrior, be of a particular economic status, have a specific kind of intellect, or belong to a specific race in order to assimilate into true manhood.

All a brother has to do is decide to level up and have the right scaffolding around him. Because no man builds his life alone.

Finally, in both illustrations, notice that it's never done alone. The Maasai warriors and Jacques Cousteau were only ever-victorious because they had proper support. They had other men who were committed to the success of their mission.

Any rite of passage into manhood necessitates the involvement of other men. But, there's a caveat to this. Let's make sure the brothers we are looking for support from are more like Johnathan was to David in the Bible than they are like Jonadab was to Amnon.

Another consideration for manhood. How we select and organize our relationships. Are the brothers on your ship and in your tribe helping you to accomplish your mission? That thing that glorifies God and improves the lives of others and is worthy of imitation? Are they helping you see more clearly? Value your treasure? And Grow in God-consciousness? Or do they aid and abet you in pulling off unthinkable foolishness?

> *When I was a child, I talked like a child, I*
> *thought like a child, I reasoned like a child;*
> *When I became a man, I did away with*
> *childish things. (1 Corinthians 13:11, AMP)*

Dr. Victor Couzens

Chapter One: Running Red Lights

"Behold, today I am setting before you a blessing and a curse– the blessing, if you listen to and obey the commandments of the Lord your God, which I am commanding you today; and the curse, if you do not listen to and obey the commandments of the Lord your God, but turn aside from the way which I am commanding you today, by following (acknowledging, worshiping) other gods which you have not known"
(Deut. 11:26-28, AMP).

Sometimes, we become accustomed to tuning things out. We push aside, ignore, and dismiss certain things, even things we really shouldn't disregard. This was me. This has been me. This is still me on some days. With every possible warning sign you could think of, I have absolutely run some red lights.

I'm not referring to that rectangular device that hangs from the electrical line at the intersections. I am talking about the red lights of my conscience, values, standards, and morals.

Whenever we ignore things that we should pay more attention to, we create unnecessary complications for ourselves and perhaps even put ourselves and others in danger.

I have never received a citation for running a red light with a vehicle. Still, I have, more times than I can count or would care to admit, disregarded blatant warning signs in relationships, whether personal, romantic, or professional, and in life, in general. At times, the consequences have been catastrophic.

As a pastor, running red lights and ignoring warning signs has sometimes caused me to make poor leadership decisions. As a parent, this has caused me to overlook things in my children that needed more of my attention and guidance. As a man, running red lights has inadvertently caused me to make unhealthy relationship decisions. As a Christian, this has even caused me to make decisions that violate the standard I'm called to live according to.

Red lights in life are those clear warning signs that indicate that we need to pump our breaks, slow down, or come to a complete stop. The thing is, no one teaches us to pay attention to the red lights in life. *Wait a minute! That sounds like blame, doesn't it?*

In life, we are the product of our decisions. There is often a temptation to blame shift when things go awry. Sometimes we blame God. Sometimes we blame others, and sometimes we blame both God and others. You can't learn from your mistakes and simultaneously neglect to accept responsibility for them. Remember, you are the one behind the wheel of your life.

Owning your decisions instead of blaming God or others is critical to growing through life's adversities versus just going through them.

I started preaching at 14 and pastoring at 19. Of course, this means all of my mistakes, errors, growth, and bad seasons have played out in a fishbowl of sorts. Over the years, I have certainly hit my fair share of brick walls in life due to my poor judgment. And or lack of maturity in certain areas. However, I could have easily avoided many collisions had I simply paid more attention to the red lights.

When public scandal, relentless rumors, and mayhem hit my life, it forced me to take inventory of my life and decisions on every level.

The reality was, I had gotten good at crossing some boundary lines and ignoring that little voice in my Spirit that at times was trying to talk me out of making yet another unhealthy decision.

Some people call it intuition, others identify it as the leading of the Spirit, and some call it a gut feeling. Whatever you call it, don't violate it! The more you violate it, the more you will become desensitized to it. I have learned this the hard way.

When we run red lights in life, we create dangerous situations for ourselves and put others at risk as well, similar to the conditions when you're in a vehicle, and you consistently tear through red lights.

Driving Under the Influence

Have you ever been under the influence? Ok, don't answer that out loud. Whenever you are under the influence, it's more probable that you will disregard and disrespect boundaries, violate agreements (even the ones you have made with yourself), and put yourself in dangerous situations.

In life, there are a variety of influences that can affect your judgment. Some of them include pain, rejection, peer or professional pressure, perception, desperation, success, ambition, popularity, and unfulfilled desires. This is only a partial list.

It is essential to know what is actually driving your decisions (we will discuss this more later). Not only does driving through life *under the influence* raise the probability of running red lights, but speeding also increases this probability. Trying to do too much, too fast, and too soon may push you through a red light.

Speeding

The first time I was married, I was divorced before I was 21. Why? Because I was trying to live life too fast. I was speeding. I hadn't taken time to understand myself and what marriage was really all about.

As a pastor, at one point, I hired a person on my staff, which turned out to be a total tragedy. Why? Because I was hurting and in desperate need of help with the team, but I was really speeding. I hadn't taken the time to vet him, check him out, get references, discuss it with people I trust, or ask better questions about his capacity. I had this idea in my mind that I needed to make something happen quickly. Had I not been speeding; the situation may have turned out differently. Eventually, I had to fire him.

On most traffic signals, the red light is preceded by a yellow light. The purpose of the yellow light is to admonish us to slow down and prepare to stop. The yellow light is the preemptive cautionary indicator that the situation is getting ready to get dangerous. We should adjust our speed and prepare to come to a complete stop. The faster we are going when the yellow light appears, the more pressure must be applied to the brakes to come to a full stop.

Distractions

Of course, there is always the element of distraction that causes us to run red lights. The driver who is not paying attention to what matters most while driving, which is happening on the road, will likely run a red light.

One of the classic place's distractions occur is in relationships. Either romantic, plutonic, professional, or otherwise.

Perhaps you can identify. There have been times in relationships when, although I knew that the relationship wouldn't last, I felt a false sense of security or fulfillment in the throes of the relationship. Although I knew full well that if I maintained the relationship, it would only cause me problems or end badly.

Ironically, no matter how many lies, inconsistencies, acts of betrayal, or questionable behavior we witness, sometimes we keep running the red lights and ignoring what we know we need to do, which may be to confront it or move on or both.

The problem? We get distracted by minor things while overlooking major issues. I admit and can identify. It is easy to become so distracted by the beauty of an apple that we fail to acknowledge the rottenness of the tree.

I mentioned a few paragraphs ago that I started Pastoring when I was 19. Once there was a couple in the church that gave very generously. In fact, they gave more financially in a year than many people give over the course of several years. It was a small ministry, participation wise, and we needed every dime we could get, so their giving was undoubtedly appreciated.

The problem is, both of them were control freaks, and they were mean. Every committee I put them on, the whole committee ended up quitting. This happened several times. When new people would join the church, this couple would find a way to run them away if they could not control them. As the pastor, I knew I needed to talk with the couple, but I was afraid that it would impact their giving if I offended them. I was running a red light. I was so distracted by their giving that I overlooked the more extensive damage they were doing to the church.

This, my friend, is how distractions work; they cause damage while creating delusion. Delusions reinforce dysfunctional decisions and undermine our best judgment.

Eventually, the couple and I did sit down and talk. Ultimately, they left the church, and to my surprise, the church did not miss a beat financially or otherwise.

The problem was, I took the posture that Adam took when God confronted him in the garden. Adam blamed God, the woman, and the serpent; he blamed everybody except for himself.

Unsuccessful people make decisions based on their current situation; successful people make decisions based on where they want to be. - Anonymous

The Power of Decisions

Ultimately, it's not the vision and desires you have for your life that leads your life; it's the decisions you make. The habits you choose will determine your success or failure in life.

Making decisions consistent with your vision for your life is part of the payment required for success. Only when your decisions are consistent with God's plan and desire for your life can you actually fulfill His divine vision and plan for you. Running red lights creates an atmosphere for avoidable collisions.

While we may not be able to control all that happens to us, we can control what happens inside us. - Benjamin Franklin

God doesn't make robots. He's not Steve Jobs; He's not programming us like computers. He gives all of us free choice, which was one of the most loving things that God could have ever done for us. However, in giving us free choice, he also lays out the consequences of our choices.

All consequences are not necessarily negative; there are also positive consequences. The definition of consequences is essentially *the result or effect of an action or a condition*.

In Deut. 11:26-28, the Lord tells us, *'if you choose to obey my commands, and follow the way that I am leading you, you're going to receive blessings. However, if you choose disobedience, you're going to receive consequences as well, but not necessarily ones that you'll be proud of.'*

God doesn't keep all things from us. Of course, He doesn't give us complete foresight and insight. But in His love and grace, He provides us with enough information, data, and intel to have a reasonable measure of predictability about how things will turn out, based in part on our choices and decisions. Unfortunately, when things don't turn out the way we would like, we generally don't consider whether we have been running red lights and violating boundaries.

Confronting and processing personal setbacks and finding the best and healthiest way to learn from them is important. But, when we get in a hurry, we don't think as clearly as we should, and we end up overreacting or under responding because we tend to either get ahead of what the situation requires or lag too far behind.

When we make mistakes, it's vital that we not cut corners in dealing with the root issues the mistakes are born out of.

We need to deliberately slow down our thought processes, responses, and perspectives to get a fuller understanding of the opportunity that has been presented to us by the chaos. Ultimately, this will discipline us and grow us in ways that are only made possible as a result of tests and trials.

How to Avoid Running Red Lights

Stay sober-minded. Don't get intoxicated with things that will impair your judgment. Taking in too much criticism will make you feel worthless and push you into darkness. Taking in too much praise will make you overestimate yourself and turn you into an arrogant imbecile. It's dangerous to operate under the influence of either of these extremes.

Try to anticipate where your decisions have the most likely probability of leading you. If your decisions and choices are not giving you the outcome you would like, the best thing to do is stop and reevaluate and figure out what course corrections are needed.

Slow down! Don't make significant, potentially life-impacting decisions on the fly. You might be surprised at how differently you see some things by simply slowing down to consider them more fully. Slowing down allows you the critical time you need to seek counsel, pray, think, ask questions and check-in with yourself.

Dr. Victor Couzens

Focus on the road ahead. There will always be things competing for your attention and focus. Don't get distracted by the stuff on the sidelines, the haters in the stands, or the cadence of another person's journey. Focusing on the road ahead will help you not miss making high-impact decisions and even minor adjustments to help you be more successful, more fulfilled, and have authentic peace.

Tell yourself the truth about what you see. When you see caution signs, yellow lights, and other warning signs, respect them, and make the appropriate adjustments. Remember, sometimes it is better to rebuild your speed because you had to slow down than recover from a crash because you didn't stop when you had the chance.

Chapter Two: Discipline is More Important Than Talent

Samuel said, "Has the Lord as great a
delight in burnt offerings and sacrifices as
in obedience to the voice of the Lord?
Behold, to obey is better than sacrifice, and
to heed [is better] than the fat of rams.
1 Sam 15:22

Arguably success in life is not determined by our talents but rather by our discipline. The discipline we bring to our talents, opportunities, and even our daily regimen is the real game-changer. Please read that again.

Discipline is the bridge between goals and
accomplishment.
- Jim Rohn

I've always been a reader and prided myself on being an intellectual and gaining head knowledge around my vocation, which, of course, is preaching. I was blessed by the opportunity to attend and graduate from three of the nation's finest institutions. All of them have helped me grow my gifts of preaching and leadership.

In retrospect getting a degree was actually a tandem goal. The complementary achievement of earning a degree is achieving and mastering some level of discipline. No one gets through multiple degree programs or accomplishes much of anything without discipline, but ironically, I've never attended an institution that offered a class on discipline.

Discipline is one of those core assets that everyone needs, but some people struggle to grasp. Personal setbacks in my life revealed to me that discipline was one the areas I needed to tighten up in. And have more respect and appreciation for.

No school has ever formally trained me to operate in discipline. That's not a knock against the institutions. It is an acknowledgment that some things can only be achieved by applying ourselves and holding ourselves accountable to the steps necessary to operate in your personal best.

What is discipline? One of the ways I define discipline is *"a consistent pattern of decisions, chosen to produce a desired result or achieve a desired goal."*

It is also the ability to forgo temporary satisfaction or gratification for the sake of long-term success or a higher goal. I don't believe that discipline is just enacting or inflicting correction or punishment in response to infractions or undesirable conduct.

There's only so much you can get from a textbook or a classroom. Most lofty goals require evaluating the missing components in one's character and maturing emotionally, not just intellectually. Discipline allows talent to endure past the initial sprint and win the marathon.

When marketers and ad agencies showcase athletes to sell clothes, shoes, fitness memberships, diet pills, etc., they often fail to mention that discipline is a significant factor in those athletes' success. In fact, many athletes with tremendous talent didn't have long-term success because they lacked discipline. We also see this in many other professions in life. Many musicians and singers who have achieved stardom could not maintain or sustain that stardom because of a lack of discipline. Yet, some people are marginally talented but freakishly disciplined and enjoy more sustained success.

Seek freedom and become captive of your desires. Seek discipline and find your liberty.- Frank Herbert

Talent is the gift given to us by God. We don't get to pick our talent; it's innate; encoded in our DNA. I believe God decided your talent before your body breached the birth canal, and your feet hit the ground.

Discipline is the Gift We Employ for the Mastery and Stewardship of Our Talents.

Remember when I said success in life is not determined by our talents but by our discipline? Here I am repeating it. Self-discipline is the real game-changer.

I think I am talented in a unique way. I have a unique ability to recall things and see things in a divergent manner. I am a gifted communicator. People have filled up rooms just to hear me speak. They have driven miles upon miles to listen to me. But at times, I have struggled deeply and profoundly with just being more disciplined. I do not say the former in an effort to brag, but instead to foster an opportunity for transparency and share what I have learned the hard way about valuing and assimilating discipline.

Talent Makes You Good, but Discipline Makes You Great.

Think about the people you know with exceptional talent. Consider the athletes, writers, musicians, entrepreneurs, artisans, intellectuals, speakers, artists, etc. that you consider successful. Now, think about those who may not be regarded as successful. Barring other factors, those who have managed to make good on the talent invested in them are very likely to have at least one thing in common: *discipline*.

It has been said that it takes 10,000 hours to become good at something. The story is told of the origins of the musical group, *The Beatles,* and how they rose to fame in England in the 1970s. Arguably, when they were just starting, they were not the most talented music group of that era. It is believed that one of the things that set *The Beatles* apart and make them great was their relentless discipline.

Many think talents alone will secure their goals and deliver their destiny. This is an unfortunate misnomer, yet there is often a concerted effort to develop talent without developing an appreciation for the discipline that talent and goals demand.

As far back as I can remember, there have been people in my life that wanted to help hone my talent. I have benefited from countless individuals' mentoring, but sometimes I overlooked the discipline patterns they demonstrated.

You must employ consistent discipline for perpetual success. Discipline manifests itself in a steady, sustained effort that refuses to get lost in the mire of non-essential matters. The moment you and I stop investing discipline is the moment things start slipping. Our health, our relationships, our careers, and so much more either rise or fall because of discipline or the lack thereof.

Discipline is such an influential factor that everything in our lives is influenced by it. And it is never far from us. Every day our lives require it. There is little that we do apart from discipline.

Here is what I have learned, the hard way about growing in discipline.

Evaluate Your Thought Processes Concerning Discipline.

Think about whether or not your current practice of discipline is moving you closer to your goals. Is your level of discipline helping you to maximize your talents, optimize your opportunities, and create the life you want? Or, is your current level of discipline hindering and eroding these things?

Several years ago, I visited my doctor for a routine physical. When the lab results came back, we discovered that I was pre-diabetic. My physician shared the news with me in a very unconventional manner. His words to me were, "You are right on track; just keep doing what you're doing, and you will be next."

I was baffled! I could not imagine what in the world he was talking about. So, of course, I asked him what I was on track for and in what way was I going to be next.

His response was certainly not what I expected.

He went on to explain that based upon my blood work, I had disciplined myself to a "sedentary, eat-whatever-you-like-whenever-you-want, stay up late, don't exercise lifestyle." I hadn't paid much attention to the fact that I'd gained nearly 30 lbs. since my last visit. He told me all I needed to do was stick with this same stratum of discipline, and I would be his next diabetic patient.

What in the world?!

Right then and there, I had to make a decision about my goals and desired outcomes for my health. If my goal was to join the diabetics ranks and the preachers with the big belly's, all I had to do was stay at the same level of discipline and do what I was already doing. However, a new goal would require better discipline.

My life was not going to change because of wishful thinking, strong desire, or prayer. My life was only going to change when my mind changed about breaking the covenant I had made with my diminished levels of discipline. My prayers needed to focus on elevating my mind to upgrade my discipline towards optimum health and a better physique.

It's essential to *set clear goals*. Get clear about what you want. Knowing what you want will help you to coalesce your efforts and your energy in a disciplined fashion.

The life you are experiencing, the type of opportunities you are attracting, and the manifestations you are realizing are reflections of your discipline. Discipline stratums are the incremental conscious decisions you make that are supported by your corresponding actions.

Discipline is time management, thought management, resource management, and self-control. It is telling yourself, "No!" at times. It is pushing yourself beyond your immediate desires in favor of the big picture.

Discipline is motivated by vision and potential positive outcomes. It is the course correction you bring to a life you know could be better, more fruitful, and more purposeful with more discipline. Discipline is uncomfortable and yet rewarding. It is intentionally making decisions that serve your end game and permitting yourself to make better decisions without feeling the need to explain or justify them.

How to Approach and Cultivate Discipline

Recognize talent as raw material, not the finished product. Value your talents and opportunities enough to employ the discipline required to get the most out of them. If you have little or limited appreciation for your talents, then you will be hard-pressed to switch out inferior discipline for superior discipline.

People who see their talents as raw material often know how to "out-discipline" their deficiencies. In many instances, deficiencies won't have the final say in your life if you employ the workaround called discipline. Discipline can compensate for deficiencies.

David Boies is an excellent example of this principle.

Boies is one of the foremost litigators in the world. He is highly sought out and extremely successful. Boies was the lead litigator in the United States' successful case against Microsoft. In 2000, *Time Magazine* named him "Lawyer of the Year."

Here's the thing. Boies was born with dyslexia. He did not learn to read until the third grade. As a child, his mother noticed that although he struggled with reading, he was very talented. His raw talent was his memory and ability to analyze the details of what he heard. His mom would read stories to him, and he would memorize the words read to him nearly verbatim and recite them back to her.

Boies disciplined himself to receive, process, and critique information in a manner that set him apart from his peers, although even as an adult, he continued to read slowly.

Demand More of Yourself

You may not have dyslexia, but whatever disadvantage or disability you believe you have can very likely be counteracted by discipline. Adjust your perception, determine your goal(s), identify your talents, and see them as raw material.

A familiar adage observes, "out of sight, out of mind." But, that's not an acceptable form of discipline.

A few months back, I asked my wife to stop buying cookies and sweets when she goes grocery shopping. One reason was that in the early hours of the morning, when I should be sleeping, I'd be in our kitchen devouring cookies and sweet treats.

My wife lovingly and supportively acquiesced to my request. She stopped buying cookies, and I felt triumphant and victorious over the snack demon, trying to take me out. However, I noticed that when I would check into a hotel, there would often be cookies on the counter, and when I flew on airplanes, they would offer me cookies, and many restaurants where I ate had cookies on the menu.

I could not very well ask every establishment that I patronized to put away their cookies. There was only one way this was going to work for me. Instead of "out of sight, out of mind." I had to discipline myself to adapt a mindset that, "although it's in my sight, it's not on my mind."

How did I do this? I had to give my goal greater prominence in my mind than the immediate gratification of the cookie. In this case, the plan was and is to maintain a certain weight and for my clothes to fit on me in a particular way.

Discipline is principally about mastering the mind and thought processes. Later in this book, we will deal more pointedly with the impact of our thoughts and worldview.

Discipline is a Mindset.

Changing the way we think will change the decisions we make. Discipline is false and superficial if it is only exercised in the absence of something. This is perhaps entirely counter-intuitive to what others suggest. In no way am I pontificating that there is no value in removing stumbling blocks or temptations from your environment. However, these things should be understood as an initial or supplemental step and not the ultimate step towards self-discipline.

Talent demands discipline, and discipline determines the capacity of your talent. I have learned the hard way that discipline must be consciously cultivated in the mind—and supported by healthy decisions.

What lies in our power to do, lies in our power not to do. - Aristotle

We live in a culture where we sometimes celebrate people's talent without giving a lot of thought to evaluating their discipline or lack thereof. Behind the scenes, we may know that some of these people don't have the discipline they need to sustain their talent, but as long as they are useful for specific purposes, win awards, make great music, etc. we celebrate them. Unfortunately, this kind of complicity perpetuates toxic cultures where people shine but do not grow.

We need organizational cultures that have high regard for discipline, not just talent.

In 1 Sam 15:22, we find a portion of the narrative between Samuel, the Prophet, and Saul, the King. It's interesting to note that Saul, by nationality, did not qualify to be the King because he wasn't from the tribe of Judah; he was a Benjamite.

God gave Saul a fantastic opportunity, and all he had to do was obey God. In other words, be disciplined. But, instead of disciplining himself with his responsibilities as a king in mind, he got caught up doing things his own way because he was more committed to pleasing the people than he was committed to his own dynamic destiny. Saul's failure, lack of discipline not only cost him his kingship. Ultimately, it caused his entire family to forfeit their inheritance.

Whatever tools you have in your arsenal for living your best life. Whatever keys of success you are working with and whatever scaffolding you are using to reach your next level. I trust that discipline is one of them.

Chapter Three: Self-Awareness; Your Personal Ph.D.

> *"Test and evaluate yourselves to see*
> *whether you are in the faith and living*
> *your lives as [committed] believers.*
> *Examine yourselves [not me]!"*
> *2 Cor. 13:5*

If you ever find yourself facing a personal setback or embarrassing situations, please remember that becoming consciously aware of how it is impacting you and what your internal options are may be more important than telling your side of the story. Or defending yourself.

During my ordeal, I faced public ridicule, became the target of bloggers, was forced to step down from an organization that I loved and cherished, and was the topic of a constant barrage of criticism. It was spiritual warfare of epic proportions.

It forced me to get in touch with myself. I had to ask myself some challenging and uncomfortable questions. "Why is this happening to me? Why are people saying these things about me? Do they really think they know me? What was it about me that created an environment for this to even take place?" These were just a few of the questions I had to consider and work through.

A firm understanding of your past and current self is essential. Experiences shape who you are and how you see the world. You can't gain self-awareness through psychology alone. Self-awareness requires a deep understanding and respect for your past and current self.

Find Your Authenticity

Self-awareness anchors your character, reveals your faith, and limits your propensity to be defined by your circumstances. It helps you uncover your authenticity.

When parts of my life became public fodder and blogger sensationalism, it naturally stirred my default defense mechanism and brought about very strong emotions. However, it took a lot of self-awareness to understand that any public defense I could give would only add to the fire.

This was a battle that had to be confronted in the realm of the Spirit, the courts of heaven, and in my own heart. Not on social media.

Proverbs tells us that a fire only continues to burn if someone continues to add wood to it, and gossip continues to ensue because people continue to participate (Prov 26:20). I had to know how my response or lack of response would add to what was occurring at that time.

I replaced my clap back with my fight back. My fight back was continuing to show up for the things that I needed to show up for and deliver in the best ways that I could. I had to face all of my responsibilities without being drawn into the "he-said, she-said." This meant I would have to conquer my impulses and be aware of my value and worth.

For a man to conquer himself is the
first and noblest of all victories.
- Plato

When it comes to self-awareness, one of the greatest gifts you can give yourself is permission, to be honest with yourself and grow in the knowledge of who you authentically are. Suppose you are not honest with yourself about yourself and are not intentional about studying yourself. In that case, you will forever be at the mercy of other people's opinions about who you are, or you will be influenced by influences such as media, entertainment, and things of that nature.

In becoming self-aware, we must challenge ourselves to make sure that we are not just facing and confronting our assets but also our potential liabilities. There will always be someone somewhere endeavoring to impose on you their interpretation of who they think you are. Sometimes, even well-intentioned people will provide insight and commentary on you. What matters the absolute most is your own thoughts and knowledge of yourself.

Do you know who you really are and what you are truly capable of......?

The Process of Self-Awareness

The process of being self-aware is perpetual. Grant it; there are some core things about each of us that are firmly intact. How it manifests will vary based upon several things.

Who you are or need to be in one season of your life may not necessarily be who you are or need to be in another season of life. You will outgrow various versions of yourself.

Your personality has dimension. Your temper has limits. Your energy has stopgaps. Your moods have filters. The way you are with your co-workers may not be the way you are with your close friends and family.

I'm a husband, a father, pastor, African American male, and more. I've had to evolve and become more self-aware of how I relate and execute all of these roles. Being aware of where you are and what you are will ultimately help you more aptly manage yourself. And serve your optimum self to others.

In learning to manage ourselves, we also have to understand that it is ok to refuse to live in the vacuum or weight of other people's perspectives, opinions, or attitudes toward us. Getting here might require you to have several meetings with yourself.

When I had and still have these self-meetings, I deliberately and sometimes painfully peel back the complicated layers of my identity without the burden of demarcation titles and lines. While asking candid questions.

Who am I? Who have I been? Who have I become? Who was I becoming? Questions, questions, questions, and more questions.

My self-awareness journey began with an understanding of my sonship in God. This revelation became the foundation of my self-awareness.

What is the foundation of your self-awareness? What are you using as the standard or the plumbline?

If you are a Christian, it most certainly should be the scriptures. If not, then you are perhaps left to the fragile and fleeting imposition of western or eastern culture.

As the Holy Spirit began to teach that sonship involves five things identity, authority, rights, responsibilities, and privileges. I began to grow in the knowledge and awareness of who I was in the eyes of God. That was when the temptation to want to sink into despair, defend, feel sorry for myself, and operate from shame and offense began to subside.

I had to get to the point where I did not let negative people tell me who I was, regardless of how they felt or what they thought about what they believed I had done.

There will always be a remnant of "legalistic bastards" in your orbit. These are people who try to suppress your identity and destroy you while believing they are doing God's work. Even though they may be or have been challenged in similar areas of their life.

Sons of God don't operate like that. Sons of God identify themselves as having the authority to execute reconciliation.

The enemy is a legalist. He will always try to blind us to our true identity. I call people who operate under legalism, legalistic bastards, not to be harsh or judgmental, but sons of God understand; It's either all grace or it's all law. Never both.

Bondage grows in the darkness of ignorance. If we are ignorant about who we are in God, then we will ultimately be in bondage to who people say we are or are not.

There were days I wanted to quit, and there were plenty of people lined up, encouraging me to give up. People sent me letters demanding I quit the ministry altogether. Some wrote me emails pressuring me to quit. Some people were bold enough to post their opinions about me leaving the church and trying to force me out of town on my social media platforms.

But growing in the awareness of who I am in God caused something amazing to happen that brought me deeper into healthy self-awareness.

Value the Journey and Embrace the Process

I believe self-awareness is your personal Ph. D. because a Ph. D. is an earned research-based degree that requires original research, data, and it expands the borders of your knowledge. In part, it is designed to either address or propose a solution to a problem.

Self-awareness is the work we do to matriculate towards a more intimate personal understanding. It's similar to earning a Ph.D. It demands self-evaluation (research), processing loads of personal data (analytics), and the expansion of the capacity of our knowledge (change, growth, maturity).

When we receive the revelation of sonship, it empowers us to put out feet on the ground and stand up in sonship and refuse to quit; not because we are perfect, but because the Father still calls us "Son," regardless of what we did or didn't do; or, what *they* said you did or didn't do!

This becomes a marvelous framework to amalgamate self-awareness from.

I have two sons and four daughters. Like many parents, I've gone through some uncomfortable, trying, and taxing seasons with my children. However, the one thing that I continuously try to make them aware of is that no matter what they do, I'm always going to be their Dad. Even if I have to adjust my parenting approach, I may not like what they did, and they may have to hear my mouth and get chastised, but no matter where they go or what they do in life, I am their Father.

As we grow in self-awareness and genuinely get in touch with who we are in the eyes of the creator, we gain a sense of liberty.

Until sonship revelation, I had never experienced legitimate self-awareness. I am not sure when I would have started on my own personal Ph.D. had I not gone through or faced the mire of circumstances and difficulties I faced.

It's important to point out that some aspects of growing in self-awareness aren't necessarily pretty, healthy, or righteous, but even the negative parts of our lives can help make us more aware of who we truly are.

Stay on the Dance Floor

Self-awareness gives us the space that we need to grow. I have come to understand that growth is not like walking a tightrope or a straight-line. Many times, growth is like the electric slide. You remember that iconic line dance from the '90s? Sometimes you go forward, then backward, or just spin around in circles. When you notice things about yourself, be easy on yourself and whatever you do, *stay on the dance floor of self-awareness!*

One time, I was invited to a rehearsal for a ballet recital. I'm not a good dancer, but what I learned was that the best dancers are open to correction. The whole rehearsal lasted maybe two hours, but at least 90 minutes of it involved the choreographer correcting the dancers, correcting their timing, cadence, poise, movements, and steps. They were under the constant scrutiny of the choreographer, who was a relentless corrector.

Finally, during the last 30 minutes of the rehearsal, the dancers performed flawlessly. However, their flawless execution of the selected pieces was only possible because they endured the correction and made the necessary adjustments.

Growing in your self-awareness involves constant correction of your thoughts, your attitude, and your perspective. This can become an exciting adventure! The key is to keep adjusting, keep stretching yourself, and stay on the dance floor of personal growth.

Finding the bedrock and foundation of your identity is crucial, but it's not the only thing that matters. Gracious acceptance is essential. You don't have to like or celebrate every part of who you are, but it's good to accept yourself graciously. When I referenced that iconic line dance from the '80s and encouraged you to stay on the dance floor, even if your moves weren't quite ready for a soul train line, this is what gracious acceptance looks like.

The goal is not perfection; it is progress

As long as you are making progress, you are headed in the right direction.

It's nearly impossible to change and recalibrate what we don't acknowledge. When you recognize the old, negative, less than stellar patterns or traits in your life as part of who you have been, accept them. But instead of taking on guilt and shame, which are principalities of darkness, simply own them and then break your agreement with them. Tell them they cannot be part of the you that you are becoming.

Personally, this helped me begin to create a safe internal space in my heart and soul where I could practice self-forgiveness and mourn over the unhealthy and outdated parts of me that I needed to release.

The public's noise was loud, but the louder the crowd's noise became, the more I learned to love myself enough to be empathetic and stay engaged with the process I had begun.

When negative feelings, rage, bitterness, or hatred would invade my mind and soul, I acknowledged the emotions. Still, I immediately seized the opportunity to admit how damaging these things would be to my future self if I held on to them. I had to recognize that these demons were out to ground me into a lesser version of who I needed to be.

Notice the words you use and pay attention to your feelings. Look for correlations in your thinking patterns. The goal is not to beat yourself up but to help you get to the root of your identity.

Are your thought patterns your own, or have you begun to mirror someone else's thinking? What is the source of your feelings? Why are they there? These are considerations to ponder to get to the root of your identity. And make progress in your thinking.

I have learned the hard way that self-awareness empowers and strengthens us. It helps us to move from the place of a cluttered and superficial identity to a more authentic us. Authenticity is one of my deepest desires for you.

You Don't Have to Figure it Out Alone

Sometimes self-awareness is a group exercise or a collaborative effort. I have benefited from the droves of people who have helped me embrace my higher identity, which is why I'm much healthier now and can offer these lessons.

I admire people who can figure themselves out all by themselves. That's not my story; I am complex, and therefore I needed the aide of others. I have been blessed to have a lot of amazing people who had a vested interest in me. Some solicited and some unsolicited. But, all well-intentioned.

I call them FEMA (Friends, Encouragers, Members of your family, and Associates).

When a natural disaster happens in America, the government activates FEMA (the Federal Emergency Management Agency). They show up to execute resources for the affected.

Sometimes no matter how hard you try, it is still difficult to remember who you are and the greatness you were born for. That's where your FEMA becomes handy. Give your FEMA permission to affirm that you are valuable and allow them to become part of your self- awareness process. Your FEMA can remind you that you are necessary, reconfirm that you are an overcomer, and help you see that you have everything you need to grow and evolve. Your FEMA will help you realize you have the power to eliminate everything standing between you and the awareness of what is required for the healthiest, more fruitful you.

Whatever you are in pursuit of, please make sure that you are carving out time to work on your most important project ever, which is your personal Ph.D.

Chapter Four: Embrace Your Humanness

But we have this precious treasure [the good news about salvation] in [unworthy] earthen vessels [of human frailty] so that the grandeur and surpassing greatness of the power will be [shown to be] from God [His sufficiency] and not from ourselves.
2 Cor. 4:7

You are not *only* human; your humanness is a vital part of your existence. However, it does not ultimately define you. In fact, being human gives you broad potential and makes you instantly valuable. Humanness is an acknowledgment and confession of your strengths and an indicator of your capacity, frailty, and needs.

What is tolerance? It is the consequence of humanity. We are all formed of frailty and error; let us pardon reciprocally each other's folly - that is the first law of nature.
~ Voltaire

Regardless of any merit or accomplishments in your life, your humanness means you need love, support, hugs, high fives, accountability, and shoulders to lean on. You are fractured and flawed, and you'll never be able to please everyone, every day. And you are hardwired to accomplish ridiculously amazing things, bounce back from adversity and excel against the most tremendous odds.

To embrace your humanness is to acknowledge these basic needs along with your unique needs. In some way or another, we all basically need the things I mentioned above and other things like affirmation, correction, guidance, rest, and so much more.

Making purposeful decisions while acknowledging who we are is not only critical, but it is healthy as well, and yet it is a learned practice. Being human requires a fair amount of emotional intelligence (also known as EQ). Balanced with the art of being conscious of your purpose and contribution to the rest of humanity. There will be things in life that will seek to diminish your role and contributions to society. When this happens, remember you have too much purpose on you to succumb to the forces set against you.

Embracing your humanness is far different from saying, "I'm *only* human." If you believe that *all you are is human,* with all you have already survived, overcome, defeated, faced, and dealt with, you are playing yourself! Don't play yourself! Although your humanness is a vital part of your existence and does not absolve us from being responsible, we are not "only human."

Some of the joy of being human includes engaging in healthy relationships, enjoying nature, participating and contributing as a part of a community, enjoying great food, listening to vinyl records, laughing, loving, playing with puppies, holding babies, and being loved, etc.

These are things that many well-adjusted adults enjoy, yet, coming to grips with the responsibilities and limitations of being human while identifying your personal, unique needs and executing your purpose is an endless chore. This is where the work of embracing your humanness comes into play.

In a treatise by a first-century tent maker, it is written, "We have this treasure in earthen vessels...." The truth is, we all have something valuable and precious inside of us. It's our responsibility to protect it, nurture it, and invest in it. There are no surrogates for this.

You will make mistakes, say stupid things, jump to conclusions, have irrational moments, endure stress, cry, struggle with insecurities, and perhaps even question your value at times.

As a human being, embracing your humanness is the permission you give yourself to authentically settle into who you are and what you offer to the world in the form of purpose. This is fundamental to high impact living. And this is what sets the framework for wholeness.

How Do We Identify Our Unique Human Needs?

One of the ways we identify our unique human needs is by observation. This may sound a tad elementary but just think with me for a minute. What are the moments or seasons in your life where you felt like you were at your personal best?

Now, shift your thinking just a little and consider the type of scaffolding you had around you. Were you in a relationship? Was it healthy? What was your meditation and prayer life like? What was your nutrition and daily regimen like? Were you staying up late/going to bed early? What kind of people were part of your tribe/village/community or inner circle at that time? What were you reading? What were you listening to? Was it before, during, or after a divorce or other major life transition?

Think about these questions. Take time to journal and write it down if you have to.

These are the kind of observations needed to hone in on your unique personal needs as a human. And the conditions under which you thrive. Owning your healthy needs is essential to purposeful living. You will always know that your needs are healthy by what they bring out of you and add to you.

Healthy human needs make us more responsible, kinder, more ethical, more moral, mentally tough, spiritually aware, and more productive. The darker and less attractive side of embracing your humanness involves processing your difficult seasons, sabotaging decisions, and uncomfortable emotions. To be human is to have both light and darkness in you. Like you and I are capable of undying love, we are also capable of foolishness, indiscretion, and even hate.

Perhaps like you, I genuinely don't want to hate. But I have had to acknowledge the presence of hate in my heart at times.

I never knew that hate was even remotely a possibility for me. Yet, every time I hear the report or see the footage of another unarmed black person murdered by the police, darkness, and hatred that I never even knew was in me begins to creep up. It's not directed towards the police or as a whole. It is directed towards the fact that African Americans are in an impossible situation in America. We are African with none of the history and Americans with none of the privileges.

Why do I wrestle with these emotions of hate that are rooted in darkness? Because I am human.

Knowing how to handle your darkness will give you the power to walk in your light. We cannot afford to be naïve about the dark side of our personalities. Being fully aware of the darkness in you is the best way to identify and respond to others' darkness.

People that embrace their humanness grieve differently, cope better, respond to conflict differently, and bounce back faster from setbacks.

What are your personal greatest needs as a human? How are these needs different from your needs 18 months ago? What are your dynamic strengths? How readily do you accept support? Criticism? Correction? What are some of the dark sides of your personality?

As a Christian, I have learned that my faith was never intended to encourage me to deny my humanness in favor of my spirituality. Instead, my faith actually gives me a place to deal with, address, and manage who I am as a human being living in a fallen world.

Even spiritually minded or deeply religious people have human urges, desires, responses, anxious moments, and negative inclinations. This should not come as a surprise, but for some reason, it often does. This issue is the contagious phenomenon of hypocrisy; many people would rather be thought to be human than proven to be human.

Finding Harmony

Harmony is different from balance. Harmony is the congruity of parts to their whole or to one another. Balance is a point between two opposite forces that is desirable over purely one state or the other. This is one of the reasons why

I absolutely love the scriptures. They advocate for harmonious humanness.

The scriptures are not only God's words; they are God's narratives and stories. He could have caused them to be written in the most fantastic and flattering way imaginable. There are things He could have flat out refused to allow to be written, and perhaps in some ways, He did. However, what He did not do was entirely gloss over some of the most intimate, vulnerable, embarrassing, scandalous, uncomfortable, dark, and infamous episodes in the lives of humans.

The Bible abounds with stories of great people who sometimes lost their way or had what I call "heavy human moments" like Peter, who denied Jesus; like David, who acted on unbridled urges; like the brothers of Joseph, who operated in jealousy; like sex worker, Rahab, who worked in an unseemly enterprise; like Naaman, who struggled with pride; and like Samson, who chose the wrong woman to keep company with. All of these real-life stories are in the greatest, most popular, best-selling book of all time. And according to Romans 15:4, they were written for our benefit and instruction.

I have had to learn the hard way to take 85% of what I thought being human was about and flush it down the toilet. No, seriously. It took a lot of reevaluation, observation, and confrontation to conclude that what I thought I understood about these things just did not consistently serve me well. So, here is what I learned the hard way about being human.

It's not good to turn your back on who you really are. Turning your back on who you really are is like locking a bear in a closet. Eventually, the bear is going to break out.

Instead, embrace who you really are, face who you really are, look for the good and the value in who you are, and align who you are with your core beliefs, values and purpose. If you are a Christian as I am, this most certainly includes allowing the Holy Spirit to produce His fruit in your life, according to Galatians 5. This is called sanctification. Sanctification brings harmony.

New Perspectives Brings New Possibilities

Here's an alternative perspective on weakness. Weakness is sometimes strength focused in reverse.

Let me give you an example.

Let's look at another guy in the Bible; King David.

The same David that had an unbridled passion for another man's wife had a righteous passion for building God a temple and recovering the Ark of the Covenant. When his desire was for another man's wife, which is sin, yet he was determined to have her, that was his strength focused in reverse. However, when his desire was determined to build God a temple, that was his strength focused in the right direction.

Desire is desire. It is neutral until we decide which way to aim it. What direction are you focusing your desires in?

Embracing your humanness means being very deliberate and conscious of how you choose to exercise self-care in every season of your life. This means giving yourself unconditional love, room to make mistakes, space to grow, and soft places to land. It means giving yourself downtime, self-care time, quiet time, and reassessment time.

It also means being brutally honest with yourself about how you are exerting and focusing your passions.

You Are NOT Defined by One Chapter of Your Life

At the risk of scrutiny, but in the interest of helping others get past unsavory chapters in their lives. I may or may not be known to have a little Apostle Peter in me. And once I had a, shall we say, semi Noah moment.

Allow me to share a very embarrassing and humiliating experience I had years ago. Now, I caution you, especially my fellow church folks, that what I am about to share will certainly not pass some people's halo test. And in no way am I condoning or justifying the following.

Consider yourself forewarned if you choose to read the next few paragraphs.

We were in Paris. We had been dating for some time, and she said it was the one place she had always wanted to visit. So, I booked the trip and off to Paris we went.

Paris is one of the most fascinating cities in the world, for many reasons. Not only was I glad to be in Paris. But I was equally delighted to be able to let my hair down. You know, relax, unwind, and chill.

One evening we found our way to the *Little Red Door* in Paris. It's a quaint little cocktail lounge in Le Marais. They have excellent music, but they are mostly known for their beverages that are a tribute to a French word or country. It's very renowned in Paris.

I felt anonymous, discreet, safe, and capable of taking in everything the *Little Red Door* had to offer the evening of our visit. My companion at the time seemed to be enjoying herself as well. We stayed there until the house lights came up and the place was closing down. By that time, I had tried nearly everything on the beverage menu at least once, and some even twice. And boy, was I feeling it.

I am what you would call a lightweight when it comes to drinking. But hey, I was in Paris after all and with a beautiful woman, throwing caution to the wind.

When we arrived back at the hotel via Uber, we were giddy, feeling those beverages from the *Little Red Door*, talking loudly and laughing at every little thing you could think of. I wasn't concerned about being a Pastor, a father, a leader, or anything else. I was a black man in Paris, having what some would consider a blast.

Unbeknownst to me, she had been video recording the entire scene on her cell phone the whole time. Later, when the relationship ended, that video of me in a less than an admirable condition was leaked to a blogger, shared online, and boy, was the judgment and criticism swift.

I had a decision to make. Deny it and run away or embrace it and face it. I chose the latter. Not that it was a moment that I am proud of. However, embracing our humanness often means owning what happens in our lives, using it as an opportunity to grow; and refusing to be shamed or defined by it.

Embarrassing, uncomfortable, and earth-shattering moments in life stand to teach us a great deal about our emotional and mental capacity. They remind us that we need boundaries, we need accountability, we need trusted relationships, we need grace, and we need to know not to be mindful of how although a mishap may not define you. It just might set you back a peg or two.

This is not a confession of pity or a ploy for sympathy. This is an acknowledgment of the fullness of who you are, just like you may have moments of profound lapses in judgment. You are hardwired, endowed by God with resilience, tenacity, fortitude, and strength as a human. Fearfully and wonderfully made in the image of God and after His likeness. This is part of your reality as a human. I have learned the hard way; mistakes have the power to turn you into something better than you were before.

When you falter, stumble, say something stupid, do something dumb or inappropriate, decide to use it to help you grow and build. But, most of all, use these things to learn more about yourself than you did before.

Mistakes are the portals of discovery
- James Joyce

Access Portals

If you yield to overindulging, you invite the bondage of addiction into your soul. If you yield to procrastination, then everything rooted in the principality of delay comes into your soul. If you yield to impulsive decisions, all kinds of challenges and issues gain access to our lives.

These things are seeds. Every seed planted wants to grow, whether it's a seed from the Holy Spirit or a seed from the forces of darkness. The more a person waters a seed, the more that seed will establish roots and grow no matter what type of seed it is.

I have learned that when we yield to the seeds that are not designed to serve us but are designed to hinder us, we unnecessarily encumber ourselves. But, when we yield to the seeds of the light, it not only glorifies God, but it also reinforces our capacity to maintain dominion over our access portals.

The enemy is a legalist. Anytime we give him conditional access to our lives, he puts a demand on our souls and the rest of our lives. This is where recklessness becomes an issue. And how habits are formed. We may go into something with one thing in mind, not realizing that the permission we give the enemy on the left will not satisfy him. He wants every part of us.

Whether you give him access through your friends, fetishes, finances, family, or flesh, he'll use any and every access point to come in and try to destroy your soul and hinder your destiny because that's his goal. When you give him access, you are helping him accomplish his goal of scheming against you! As humans, we must know what areas of our lives we are most vulnerable in. Having this knowledge helps us become more vigilant in controlling those portals.

In Rom. 8:26, Paul says, "So too the [Holy] Spirit comes to our aid and bears us up in our weakness; for we do not know what prayer to offer nor how to offer it worthily as we ought, but the Spirit Himself goes to meet our supplication and pleads in our behalf with unspeakable yearnings and groanings too deep for utterance."

I love the fact that we have help. Even in our weaknesses and human frailty, we are not abandoned. The enemy sends cameras, critics, and crowds to exploit our vulnerableness, but the Holy Spirit comes to our aid with covering compassion and intercession.

In Gen. 2:15-17, God establishes boundaries for Adam and Eve. "*So, the Lord God took the man [He had made] and settled him in the Garden of Eden to cultivate and keep it. And the Lord God commanded the man, saying, 'You may freely (unconditionally) eat [the fruit] from every tree of the garden; but [only] from the tree of the knowledge (recognition) of good and evil you shall not eat, otherwise, on the day that you eat from it, you shall most certainly die [because of your disobedience].'*"

Satan soon came along and encouraged the first humans to scrutinize God's prohibitions, and once they begin to scrutinize God, there his minds began to shift towards fallenness. Please note that Satan was first given access to take dominion over them when they started to doubt. Doubt is an access portal that must be closely watched

> "*Now the serpent was more crafty (subtle, skilled in deceit) than any living creature of the field which the Lord God had made. And [a]the serpent (Satan) said to the woman, "Can it really be that God has said, 'You shall not eat from [b]any tree of the*

garden'?" ²And the woman said to the serpent, "We may eat fruit from the trees of the <u>garden</u>, ³except the fruit from the tree which is in the middle of the garden. God said, 'You shall not eat from it nor touch it; otherwise you will die.'" ⁴But the serpent said to the woman, "You certainly will not die! ⁵For God knows that on the day you eat from it your eyes will be opened [that is, you will have greater awareness], and you will be like God, knowing [the difference between] good and evil."
(Gen. 3:1-6).

What Adam didn't understand was that God's prohibitions are always for our protection. So, whenever God tells us, "No," it's because He's protecting us from something. He's not holding out on us. It's not that He doesn't want us to enjoy life. He knows what He has made us of as humans, and He is intimately aware of what we require.

Our lives as human beings are a very complicated matter and involve much "on the job" training. Every day we learn more about ourselves and how we relate to the world we live in.

Accountability

Accountability is one of those things that every human requires but may struggle to embrace. Accountability is a positive thing, and it reveals how committed we are to our goals and having healthy souls. Accountability increases our chances of overall success, broadens our support system, and helps maximize our opportunities.

We were created to thrive under accountability. Genesis 2:18 proves this. Where it is written, "it is not good for man to be alone." This was not just for the sake of our human need for companionship. Humans, for sure, need companionship. We need the emotional, spiritual, and psychological influence and companionship of others. We also need a culture of accountability.

Sharing your goals with trusted people, exposing your potential to others, and working on teams with others. And even transparently revealing our scars to others fosters the accountability we need to live into our best selves.

Although the journey of life may be lonely at times, we never really travel alone. And we do not succeed alone. We are the product of the accountability we have embraced or shunned because accountability helps promote our optimum potential.

The best accountability situations help us identify and be cautious of our blind spots. They challenge how we process things and our overall world view. Accountability puts us in regular touch with our goals and reminds us of the big picture.

Accountability is interpersonal. It is intentional submission to others, which is precisely part of what we need to embrace our humanness fully.

Chapter Five: Your Life is Bigger Than You

*"Next to them, Zadok son of Immer made
repairs opposite his house. Next to him,
Shemaiah son of Shecaniah, the guard at
the East Gate, made repairs."*
Nehemiah 3:29

Our lives are inextricably connected to others. There is a reverberating effect on our selections, decisions, habits, etc. Defeated people live with only themselves in mind. Successful people live in the understanding that their lives are an intricate tapestry woven with others.

Sometimes, we don't see the amalgamation of every part of our life. Personally, it took me a minute to appreciate the fact that any given aspect of my life was ultimately going to impact every other part of my life and everyone in my life. The relationships may be different. But the impact is often unavoidable. Try as hard as we please to compartmentalize the hats we wear. But there will usually be some overlap.

Unintended Impact

Parents know all too well the difficulty of making adult decisions that you don't necessarily want to explain to your child or want them to be part of. There are few things more uncomfortable as a parent than having to explain your adult decisions to your child.

All of my children live in the same media-saturated world as we all do. So, sheltering them from all the unflattering things said about me was simply impossible. This is where I learned just how interconnected every part of our lives is.

My youngest daughter and I are similar in our personalities. Our birthdays are a week apart. When I started wearing dreadlocks, she began wearing dreadlocks. When she didn't want to fly on a plane by herself as an unaccompanied minor, I booked a ticket to fly with her. She doesn't like to admit it but, she is a daddy's girl.

Because of things she read about me on social media, she began to question how I felt about her, her sisters, her mom, her aunties, her grandmothers and every other female in our family. Having to have this conversation with her was necessary but very uncomfortable.

She expressed herself to me in a letter. A considerable part of the letter was her wondering what she should expect from a man and how she would be able to trust man if what people were saying about me, her father was true. She had it in her mind that I was unkind and indifferent towards women. Although she is a teenager. One day she would be considered a woman.

Our conversation helped to shape my understanding about unintended consequences even more. Although we make decisions in a silo about who and what we bring into our lives. There are times when the fall out of these selections are more far reaching than anticipated.

No part of my life only impacts me. Every area of my life, every relationship, every decision, and every opportunity will affect someone else in my life. The same is true of you.

It took me having that hard conversation with my daughter and hearing the pain and concern in her voice to drive this revelation home.

Of course, I assured her of my love and respect for her and her sisters in my conversation with her.

No Lone Rangers

Our culture arguably thrives on the mantra of individuality and isolation. This is one of the most dangerous fallacies of our time. We are encouraged to be recklessly selfish. Our successes and missteps either serve as an asset or a liability to the communities we belong to.

One of the many lessons I learned the hard way about my life being bigger than me is the inequity of being perpetually naive about my influence on those who look up to me and are connected to me, along with the mutual impact we have on one another.

One of the things that I think I have in common with many pastors is that I'm very private. I'm an ambivert. Many of my colleagues and close friends identify as being ambiverts as well.

For me, when life gets heavy and situations and circumstances seem insurmountable, a part of my personality wants me to shoulder it alone. However, in realizing that my life is more significant than me, I have also learned that I have more help and more support than I sometimes acknowledge. And there is no need to be a lone ranger in every situation.

Living with the understanding that our lives are bigger than us helps us be mindful of how we impact others and are impacted by others.

Better Together

One of the biggest lies that the enemy tells us, especially in dark times, is, "You don't have anybody. You're in this all by yourself." When we accept and believe this, we end up living unto ourselves, in isolation depriving ourselves of community fellowship and love, even in scripture. Nearly everyone the Lord called He gave them someone to journey with and to sharpen them.

We benefit from the companionship and deposit others make in our lives. And we bless others by providing companionship and deposits into their lives. Together is very "counter-cultural." However, together is necessary for collective wisdom, group motivation, and support. In our "just do you" culture, "together" is not always appreciated.

If you want to go fast, go alone; if you want to go far, go together – Unknown

This is one of the reasons the scriptures largely reflect and endorses being part of community.

You and I belong to a community. We have the opportunity (and responsibility) to inspire and influence others and think about the impact of things in our lives on the people who are part of our lives. Embracing this is a mark of greatness.

The greatness of a man is not in how much wealth he acquires, but in his integrity and his ability to affect those around him positively. - Bob Marley

Many people desperately long for the opportunity to contribute to something beyond themselves. The good news is, you don't have to be an astrophysicist, a king, a university president, or a celebrity to influence others. All you have to do is refuse to whittle your life down to the thimble of your personal feelings, desires, or ambitions. To do so would only make you claustrophobic.

Have you ever thought about the fact that some people draw strength just from the mention of your name? You ever considered how your presence brightens someone's day. Did you know you have inspired people in untold ways? And God uses you to answer people's prayers?

Imagine how unfulfilling life would be if the great scientist George Washington Carver kept his science genius to himself. Imagine how delayed the civil rights movement might have been had Rosa Parks decided to move to the back of the bus. Now, think about how we have mourned the life of people that many of us have never met—celebrities like Whitney Houston and Chadwick Boseman. And non-celebrities like Tamir Rice and John Crawford, III. Why do we feel this connection to these people? It is because we are all interconnected.

Committing to live your life with this revelation will add more joy and a deeper depth of appreciation to your life. Live your life, being fully conscious that your presence can brighten someone's day. Some people thrive on your input, pine for your affirmation, become strengthened by your victories and receive inspiration because of your ambition. Conversely, if you are cynical, critical, unkind, messy, drama-filled, and problematic, you will attract and foster others' same traits.

This doesn't mean that you should live under the perpetual paranoia of what others think. However, it does mean that you must consider who will be impacted by your "yes" and by your "no." Knowing that others are looking to you is great motivation! However, knowing that you have people who support you helps take the pressure off.

> **What counts in life is not the mere fact that we have lived. It is what difference we have made to the lives of others that will determine the significance of the life we lead. – Nelson Mandela**

Chapter Six: Finding Purpose in Problems

"Consider it pure joy when you encounter
trials of many kinds." *James 1:3*

Problems can be the platform and catalyst for great things. But only when they are correctly processed and seen as an opportunity, not just opposition. Taking this opportunity approach helps us not miss the way our problems can serve and help us. And protect us from becoming bitter, sinking into despair, and filled with rage. Problems even have the power to turn you into something better than you were before.

Inside of every problem is an opportunity.
—Robert Kiyosaki

I have never met a person that liked problems. But I have also never met a person who has not experienced any issues or problems. Problems are inevitable, and they are varied.

Problems shake our world, sometimes disturb our lives' delicate balance, and sometimes expose us to immense pain. Problems, issues, challenges come in many different forms and for a multitude of reasons. Yet, every problem serves a purpose and provides an opportunity.

Teach us a lesson, provide correction, reinforce truth, or expose a weakness. These are just a few of the purposes of problems. It's not if we face difficulties. It's when we face problems. Having a prescribed lens through which we evaluate our challenges or problems will help us never waste a problem, but instead discern purpose concerning our problems. Sometimes problems are purpose opportunities in disguise.

Teach Us a Lesson

I have a scar on my left hand. It's a keloid scar, and it is about an inch long. I have had this scar since I was about nine years old. Right above my wrist, nearly in line with my pointer finger, is the scar. The scar shouldn't be there. I wasn't born with this scar. I earned this scar. Not in a badge of honor kind of way. But in a hard-headed mannish kind of way.

My grandfather, Willard Couzens, was my hero. He was born in 1908. He lived for 98 years. You name it, and my grandfather could do it. He was a renaissance man.

One summer afternoon, he and two of my uncles were laying some carpet. I had one job, stay out of the way, and do not touch anything. Simple enough, right?

If only I had listened, I wouldn't have this scar. I stood back and watched how they cut the carpet, stretched it out, tucked under the baseboards, and pushed into place.

Simple enough. Well, at 9, of course, I wanted to give it a try. But my grandfather had been emphatic with me about not touching anything.

When they took a break to eat lunch, I rushed in to try my hand at it. The problem was I really had no clue what I was doing, and I had already been warned.

My curiosity nearly literally cost me my hand. With my left hand pressed into the carpet, the carpet cutter in my right hand, I dug into the carpet with the carpet cutter and started to make my cut. Unexperienced and underestimating the sharpness of the blade. Faster than I could blink, blood was gushing everywhere. I had cut at least half an inch into my hand.

Today, the scar reminds me to listen to, accept, and respect wisdom, especially when it comes to foreign things to me. However, the moment has long passed. The scar serves the purpose of admonishing and teaching me that a voice of experience is more credible than personal curiosity.

Provide Correction

Admittedly some things have to come to a head in our lives before we have an Ephinay or get the real motivation to make some correction. Unfortunately, we just don't make some necessary changes and adjustments to our lives until the crap hits the fan. Sometimes correction is the purpose of a problem. God knows just where we have to bump our head to knock some sense into it.

It was three days before Christmas, 1990. My Dad came into my bedroom around 9 AM that Saturday morning. He said he was going to lay in my bed and take a nap. I remember thinking how odd it was for him to be taking a nap in the morning and in my bed, no less.

I went into him and my mom's bedroom to watch cartoons with my siblings. Several minutes passed, and I decided to go back to my bedroom to check on my Dad. As soon as I entered my bedroom, I could tell something was wrong. His jeans were soiled in the front, and his eyes were partially closed, and the part you could see were bloodshot red. Immediately I tried to wake him up. He could not be roused.

Hearing the commotion, my mom came into the room. She grabbed my Dad by the arm, and all of his weight fell back onto my bed. She screamed at the top of her lungs. Yelling, crying, and frantic, she told me to call 911.

The problem is, we did not have a phone, and this was before the wide availability of cell phones.

I ran down the stairs of our apartment bare feet, still in my pajamas from the night before. A tee-shirt and some sweatpants. Flung the apartment door open and stepped out into the cold winter air and the freshly fallen three inches of snow that came the night before.

I ran as fast as I could to get to that payphone at the corner store to call 911. By the time I ran back to our apartment, I could hear the sound of the emergency vehicles approaching.

My father was an addict at the time. He had overdosed on pills. By God's grace, the doctors were able to revive him. I ended up with second-degree frostbite on both of my feet. The overdose experience and nearly losing his life and family began my Dad's journey to sobriety. It served as the segue to the course correction my Father needed to break the stronghold.

It brought the secret of my Dad's addiction out of the closet. Forcing him to face it. While exposing his addiction to his friends and family who were able to help provide the support correction and accountability (there's that word again), the situation required.

> *Not everything that is faced can be changed. But nothing can be changed until it is faced. - James Baldwin*

Reinforce Truth

Truth that has not been proven is a theory. Few things grow us, test what we believe to be true, and tears down the lies we believe truth like problems.

When I speak of truth, I do not speak of truth abstractly or subjectively. I speak of truth in the fashion of things that we absolutely must believe and live by.

On August 29, 2005, Hurricane Katrina ravaged the gulf coast. It had a category 3 rating on the Saffir-Simpson Hurricane Scale. With sustained winds of 100-140 mph and stretched nearly 400 miles. While the storm was devastating, it was the levee's breaching and the massive flooding that produced unprecedented damage.

I have several friends and even some relatives that live along the gulf coast. One of my friends had just opened a business, another had just purchased a home, and another had recently purchased a new car for his wife.

Hurricane Katrina is arguably the single most devastating hurricane in my lifetime. Within a couple of weeks of the storm, several church members loaded up and drove to Gulf Port, Mississippi. There were no words to describe the level of devastation we observed. Buildings decimated; trees strewn about. Graves were even unearthed because of the storm surge.

For a full week, we helped clean up, served meals, passed out goods, held prayer services, and tried to support every way we could, although the devastation was fierce. The people we encountered had different reactions for different reasons.

My friend, who had just opened a business. Thankfully the building was spared, and his personal property did not have any damage, either. However, he was despondent because one of his business partner's mom died in the hurricane.

Reggie, the one who had just purchased a home. The home was flooded out, totally underwater. His furniture had floated several miles away from his home and ended up on top of a small building by the time the water receded. But, to talk to Reggie, you would not know that he had lost his home and all of his possessions in that hurricane. He was jovial and humorous when I spoke to him on the phone.

His first grandchild was born two days after the hurricane.

Although problems are inconvenient and sometimes even unfair, they do not leave much superficiality in most people. Problems sober us to the things in life that matter the most, the most important relationships, and reinforce the truth of what life is really all about.

Problems challenge us to revisit simple but sometimes overlooked truth. Things like our lives not being valuable because of the abundance of our possessions (Luke 12:15). Truth like what's in your heart is more important than what's in your driveway. Truth like, we really don't need as much as we think we do in order to be ok. Truth like the human Spirit is beautifully resilient. Problems reinforce truth.

Expose Weakness

We all have them. Even if we do not readily acknowledge them, some have more than others. They are called weaknesses.

I have this neat little hardtop convertible. It was a gift to myself after I completed my doctoral studies. Living in the Midwest only allows me to let the top down on the convertible a few months a year. And when I let the top down, I like for my ride to be clean, tires shining, windows smudge-free, and freshly vacuumed.

This little BMW gets a fair amount of attention, especially when the top is down and the two-tone color seats are clearly visible. On top of this, the car has a lot of horsepower. Shift the gear while you're accelerating, and you can top 100 mph quickly.

The car is perfect, except for one thing. Whenever I take it through the drive-thru carwash, I always notice a few drops of water get inside the car. Right where the windshield and the top connect. It's not a lot, but it's there, and it happens every time without fail. From the outside looking in, you'd never knew this is occurring. Even if you're a passenger in the car and we drove through the carwash. You would very likely not even notice the few little drops of water that enter the vehicle.

The pressure from the carwash exposes the weakness in the seal between the windshield and the convertible top.

This is what problems do for us. They reveal what would otherwise be considered perfect conditions.

The pressure of problems brings us face-to-face with where our lives' weaknesses and vulnerabilities are. Problems expose the weaknesses in our faith. The shortcomings of our values, morals, personalities, mental toughness, decision making, relationships, and ethics are revealed against the backdrop of problems.

Taken together, this is why we should and can face our problems with joy. Knowing there is a purpose to them, and knowing that every experience has value to it. Sometimes problems are purpose opportunities in disguise.

Chapter Seven: Nothing Stays the Same Forever

"There is a season (a time appointed) for everything and a time for every delight and event or purpose under heaven—A time to be born and a time to die; A time to plant and a time to uproot what is planted. A time to kill and a time to heal; A time to tear down and a time to build up. A time to weep and a time to laugh; A time to mourn and a time to dance." Eccl. 3:1-4

If you want something new, you have to stop doing something old.
— Peter Drucker

Consistency and predictability are novel. They have merit to them, but they can also provide a false sense of security. Why? Because nothing stays the same forever.

When we rely too heavily on consistency and predictability, we sometimes begin to take things for granted. Or bring things to a close whose season has ended, and time has passed. The spirit of discernment and the Spirit of wisdom empowers us to anticipate, respond to, and prepare for change.

In life, change is inevitable and sometimes is even thrust upon us. Nothing stays in one continual state indefinitely. Think about it. Hair thins, footsteps get slower, interest and taste shift, clothing goes out of style, technology becomes antiquated, people come, people go. Throughout life, we will all experience many kinds of transitions. Transitions come in different ways, sometimes as changes in marital status, work, physical health, location, the world, and our world.

When change catches us by surprise, boy, oh boy, can it be tough to deal with?

Looking back, my entire life changed in the course of a week. In some places, I had become a household name for all of the wrong reasons. Some of the people who had told me repeatedly to my face, "I'm with you to the end," decided the end had come for them. My once very full calendar dried up. Some relatives were hesitant to acknowledge that we were related. News reporters were knocking on my front door and calling my office. I was the daily discussion of church gossip bloggers. And going to certain places in public became something I had to contemplate deeply. The warfare was deep. It was intense, and it was heavy.

Never in my life did I think I would live to see anything like these things. A few months before this, I stood on a national stage at one of our premier conferences and delivered the opening message. My how quickly things had changed.

Let me tell you. I prayed, cried, complained, cried, cursed, prayed some more, cried some more, complained some more, and even cursed some more. But guess what? Change was happening, and it did not need my permission!

The walls seemed like they were caving it. Too much was happening way too fast. It was beyond my control. I had to learn to honestly and quickly evaluate my level of control in every area. I had to take my sights off of what I absolutely could not control and focus on what I could control. Once I shifted my focus, I immediately felt a lessening in the amount of anxiety I was experiencing. Thus, approaching the entire situation differently.

Change requires choices. We can either try to learn to cope with the change. We can complain and lament about the change. We can deny that change is happening, or we can participate and become invested in the change. All of the aforementioned was a possibility for me, and each had its various pros and cons.

Sometimes we choose change, and
sometimes change chooses us
- Victor Couzens

Let's go back to one of the most significant factors in change; control. Most of us are more comfortable being in control, even if we are out of our depth. When we feel like our personal control is being taken from us, it plays against our value and esteem. Learning to empower ourselves during swift and even chaotic periods of change and transition is one of the best gifts we can ever give ourselves. Even when we must empower ourselves to let go.

Be Grateful

Shake, that's what I called him. He called me Vik-tor. We had been friends for years, even though he was old enough to be my father.

I looked at the clock in my car and realized that Shake and I had been on the phone for seven straight hours. I called him a few hours into my drive from Miami to Atlanta, trying to get out of the way of Hurricane Irma. We were accustomed to talking for hours on end, but never seven hours.

We talked about sports, politics, guy stuff, scripture, and how we were going to take a group of people to the Holy Land in 2018. He was excited, and so was I. We were going to walk and teach where Jesus walked and taught.

Seven days after that, seven-hour conversation. He and his daughter drove down from Detroit because he had to minister in Dayton, OH. I went up to hear him speak in

Dayton. Even then, I could discern change was on the horizon. But I could not quite put my finger on it.

Five days later, I got the call; Shake had died. I was shocked. I was hurt. I wasn't ready. I didn't see it coming. We were just on the phone, we had just seen each other, we were just talking about taking a group to the Holy Land, and now, my brother was gone!

The swiftness of change should provoke us to be deeply grateful for every blessing: every healthy relationship and every good thing. Gratitude is essential in navigating change. Especially when the change induces grief. Being grateful empowers us and permits us to see things in their fullness and not just in their finality, especially when some kind of end comes. Gratitude helps us focus on all of the good and positive. Not just the moment of separation or loss. Instead of complaining and lamenting over the change. Be grateful that the moment, experience, or relationship ever even existed.

Both science and scripture tell us that grateful people are more resilient and handle change better. I have learned the hard way not to take the blessings of good health, good fortune, good relationships, and so on for granted. Never delay celebrating when things are going well. Live with gratitude every day.

The fact that nothing stays the same forever should only push us to depths of ridiculous gratitude and unbridled hope. Solomon's words in Ecclesiastes remind us that it is wise to make sure we maximize every desirable season and don't settle too deeply into any uncomfortable season. And in every season, be grateful.

When situations in life take a turn, when loved ones die, the company downsizes, you get laid off, or whatever the case, remember, change is par for the course. Be grateful nevertheless. Grateful for the life of the loved one, grateful the company ever even existed, and grateful for the opportunity given to even have the job.

Start in the Middle and Work Your Way Out

I'm a divergent thinker, and I'm always trying to see the other side of the coin. At times, this is good. At other times, it's not so good. I have learned, it's a good thing to be conscious of your thought processes amid change.

The tendency to overthink change or underestimate change are not the only available possibilities. Here's the thing. Sometimes it's best to start in the middle, somewhere between overthinking and underestimating. In other words, start with your neutral thoughts about change. You don't have to immediately rate it as good or bad. Give yourself a minute to process. Although, everything you think is real, everything you think is not always true.

When the gravitas of change finds your address, you might be tempted to see things in black and white instead of making mental space for the gray possibility. Dealing with and acknowledging the gray actually helps you connect with the gray matter in your brain. This is where our muscle control, sensory perception, self-control, decision making, and even emotions lie.

Things are not always as bad as they seem. Nor are things always going as well as we tell ourselves they are. Starting in the middle of my thoughts is where I was able to connect with my resilience. I had to become mindful of gray being an option.

A conscious approach to starting in the middle and not immediately declaring that the change is good or bad regulates our default tendency to overreact or become overwhelmed. Just starting in the middle and acknowledging that change is happening helped me cope with the tidal wave of sweeping changes in my life.

You don't have to get in a hurry to demonize or celebrate the change. Nor should you. You can't judge all seasons while you're in the season. Some seasons are judged through the windshield and some through the rearview mirror.

Don't Avoid or Deny the Grieving Process

In all change, there is some measure of loss. And therefore, usually, something to grieve. Change jobs, and you will probably lose contact with some of your previous co-workers. Change the operating time of your business, and you will perhaps lose a few customers. Although those two examples may indeed have some positive benefits to them, the losses can still sadden you.

Sometimes, growth comes through grief. Taking ownership of the fact that you are in mourning empowers you to give proper closure to changing seasons. Dodging the grief is akin to trying to peel your skin off. It's futile and causes more pain.

Hard times won't last forever. The difficult moments won't always be there.

In our minds, we sometimes lament when seasons change or enter into new cycles. Without recognizing that every cycle is necessary, and so is every season. We need the season of planting, and we need the season of uprooting. We need the season of laughter, and we need the season of grief. And we will laugh in some seasons and cry in others. Acknowledging the emotions associated with different seasons is permitting yourself to be present, not aloof.

In March of 2020, COVID-19 ravaged and upended the world. Particularly the USA in some very profound ways. Months upon months of quarantine. Few industries were left unimpacted, including the church. In one fell swoop, the church was thrust shoulder-deep into the digital age, and cyber sanctuaries became an actual thing. The season of large conferences, multiple services, and touch your neighbor vanished like a thief in the night. We all know that there are some things we will never get back to. This causes us grief. But we also know that some of the things which ended we should have given up much sooner.

Participate and Become Invested in the Change

Knowing that you will have to let go of certain seasons is an excellent framework for successfully navigating change. You give yourself the chance to participate in the change. Participating and becoming invested in changing seasons is a pure boss move. Although some seasons change abruptly, some seasons change gradually. When it happens this way, there are a few things you can look for to discern that a season is getting ready to change, has already started to change or when you need to force a change.

Stagnation is an indication that a season is nearing the end of a cycle. Conflict, changing dynamics, lack of fulfillment and discontent are also sometimes indications that a season is nearing the end of a cycle. The manifestation of unhealthy outcomes, loss of purpose, lack of sustainability, failure to improve, diminishing value, and low ROI are some but not all of the signs that something has shifted and preparing to come to an end.

In these instances, the atmosphere is ripe to be proactive and invest in change. While at the same time, preparing for the next season.

We participate and invest in the change in several ways. One is by preparing for what is coming. Go ahead as you can in advance and prepare yourself and your life for the new season.

Every year around late February or early March, I start making sure the blade is sharp on my garden pruners. I start walking my property, looking for bare spots on the lawn. I schedule to have the lawn sprinklers serviced, and I start stocking up on weedkiller. Why? Because we know in a few short weeks, winter will give way to spring, and things that had been dormant will begin to flower, blossom, and bud.

Because I know spring is coming, and I can see the cycle of winter coming to an end, I go ahead and start participating and investing in the season that is undoubtedly on the way. Not only by preparing but also by anticipating what the season will require. I call this Conscious consideration.

Every time a season in your life changes, your conscious consideration should stay in step with it. For example, you probably cannot live in your 40s the way you lived in your 20s. Your financial responsibilities are probably different. Your nutrition and rest needs are probably different, as well. Checking in with yourself and asking yourself questions such as, "Am I bringing what I need to where I am?" "Am I giving myself the best possible chance to win?" "Am I showing up for what this moment needs from me?" Will help you and I stay accountable to the season at hand.

You must always ask yourself, "What does this season require of me? What corrections and adjustments should I be making?"

An airline pilot once told me that 90% of flying is course correcting. The pilot and on-board system do more course-correcting while in flight than anything else to keep the plane on track. So, we have to ask ourselves, "What course corrections do I have to make to meet the demands of where I am?"

Seeking the wisdom of others is another way we participate in changing seasons.

Whatever you face in life. The death of a parent. Relocating to a new city. Experiencing a loss of income or a job. Change in relationship status. Becoming a parent. Getting a promotion. Facing the consequences of bad decisions. Somebody somewhere has faced it, gone through it, and overcome it. Soliciting their input may help you in navigating the new territory.

Intentionally participating and investing in change instead of denying or becoming ambivalent will help you calm your stress reaction. Change can be stressful, which is all the more reason to be intentional about handling it.

When we are in denial or resistant to change, we create neurochemical chaos in our brains. This causes us to overthink and become hypersensitive, which results in us spiraling out of control or sinking into depression.

Which brings me to my final observation about participating and investing in change. Prayer and professional therapy. Prayer is spiritual. Professional therapy considers the scientific realities of brain composition and human behavior. These go together like a hand a glove.

Time and space will not accommodate the time truly needed to unpack all of the benefits of prayer. However, let me insert this for your consideration.

In Luke Chapter 11. The disciples of Jesus ask Him to teach them how to pray.

This request comes near the end of Jesus's ministry on earth. Jesus had spent a considerable amount of time schooling the disciples on what to expect after his death and resurrection. There would be challenges, persecution, opportunities, misunderstandings, trouble, chaos, miracles, signs, wonders, war, tribulation, blessings, and so much more. But, most of all. Jesus, as they knew him, would not be there with them. The Holy Spirit, whom they were not familiar with, would be there, but not Jesus.

Their response, "You got to teach us how to pray." Catch this. Of all of the things they could have requested. They asked the Lord to teach them to pray. They were facing change–big changes. Significant changes. Prayer would not only keep them in touch with the Lord. Prayer would give them access to all of the wisdom, strength, courage, fortitude, resources, guidance, and help they would need.

Prayer is both proactive and reactive. It helps your strength grow, and it helps you grow in strength. Prayer releases angelic assistance and heavenly help. It positions us with the discernment we need to see things beyond the natural realm. We will get a little deeper into this in the next chapter.

I believe instead of them asking the Lord to teach them how to catch more fish, attract more people, contend against the Romans, and do all sorts of other important and significant things. Their request to be mentored in the discipline of prayer was very insightful on their part. It was intentional, and it was unconventional. Yet they knew that prayer is the primary thing in all things. Prayer is the common denominator in every major faith system (religion).

Prayer is the one thing that can get you everything - Victor Couzens

Even science testifies of the importance and impact of prayer. Prayer should be seen as part of your strategy to navigate life and to navigate change.

Responding and preparing for change *within* yourself is not the same as preparing for and responding to change *by* yourself. There are some things in life that we simply cannot confront by ourselves because we all inherently have certain blinders, finite thinking, and there's a measure of naïveté about things that most of us carry. This is where a professional therapist can become a valuable ally.

A good professional therapist will help you dig deeper into your non-conscious mind and become insightful about preparing for and responding to change. This is accomplished by mentally switching on genes that are activated through self-emergence. The human brain produces around 810,000 cells a second. Some of these cells are influenced by the quality of our thoughts, critical thinking, and even prayer. When these cells are produced in a conscious energy field of empathy, kindness, and love, they are expressed much differently than when they are produced under stress, duress, and even fear. Quality brain cells help us embrace and process change differently.

A therapist doesn't necessarily have all of the answers about everything that concerns us. However, they are often able to assist us in deconstructing change.

It's perfectly acceptable to seek existential and even professional assistance to grow in awareness and understanding of your non-conscious and conscious decision-making. This frees you from becoming a slave to your personality's deeply encoded aspects that can set you up to stumble over yourself. We often demand honesty from others when we are least honest with ourselves.

Chapter Eight: Let it Go

"Forget the former things, do not dwell on the past" Isaiah 43:18 NIV

You can't live your best life until you first die to your current life and are willing to let some things—especially things like offense, hurt, and pain. Pain is one of the many things that connect us as human beings. We all experience pain. What makes the difference is how we handle the pain.

Moving forward in a growth-orientated manner requires us to employ best practices when letting go of pain, disappointment, offense, guilt, unforgiveness, pride, lack of confidence, etc. While we can learn many valuable lessons from these things, we cannot harbor them in our emotions. Not learning to let go only prolongs the pain and suffering.

We need to let go of haunting voices of shame, crippling relationships, covenant agreements with laziness, irresponsibility, and disfunction. These are things we cannot afford to hold on to. We must neglect the strength we might be providing them.

When we don't give a fitting farewell to the things mentioned above, they impair our emotions and jade our worldview.

I learned something unflattering about myself. I was really fantastic at holding on to bad situations. Yep, I was. Sometimes holding on is very comfortable because it's familiar, but you can't get everything you're supposed to have and hold onto everything you currently have.

At any given time in life, there will be things you have to bring to an end and let go of. Dr. Henry Cloud calls them *Necessary Endings.* Whether it's a relationship, business venture, career, employee, or even long-standing associations. At times, there are things that you absolutely must let go of.

Letting go of somethings creates the necessary space for other things.

> *One can choose to go back toward safety*
> *or forward toward growth. Growth must be*
> *chosen again and again; fear must be*
> *overcome again and again.*
> *—Abraham Maslow*

We invite and create a setting for all types of problems in our lives when we keep what we should release.

For certain, the grace of God is vast, and the love of God is plentiful. Yet, there are consequences to not letting go quickly and completely. In my preface, I said everything that happened was mostly because I was disobedient. I waited far too long to let some things go. Ok, let's unpackage that a little here.

I went through a nearly two-year cycle of public shame and personal setbacks. No part of my life was unaffected. My ordeal was my fault, and I had to sit with myself and own that it was my fault. How? Because I was the one that was running the red lights, blatantly violating my conscience and the wisdom of God, and holding on to what I needed to let go of.

It was more than a delay. It was rebellion. Delaying letting go and rebelling coupled together granted conditional access to the enemy. By simply not letting go, I created an atmosphere and environment for the enemy to exploit my life and usher warfare and judgment in on me. Sometimes we deceive ourselves into believing that we are not the real problem, and, at times, we are not; however, at other times, we definitely are the problem. Especially when we live defiantly by holding on to things we are being called to let go of.

The person that manages their money poorly and is always broke is the problem. The person who refuses to exercise, eats poorly, and suffers from gout and hypertension, is the problem. The believer who lives in disobedience and then finds hell being released in his or her life; is the problem.

It's not the bills, the lab results, or the warfare. It's the person. I was my problem; I just would not let certain things go! Can you relate?

Letting go means to come to the realization that some people are a part of your history, but not a part of your destiny.
— Steve Maraboli

Everything in life has a means of elimination. Our body has a means of eliminating waste. Our automobiles have a means of eliminating exhaust. We must have a let it go strategy for our lives.

Are you creating perfect storm conditions in your life through rebellion and disobedience and holding on? Had I simply not delayed coming into agreement with God and what He had put in my consciousness, it would have probably saved many people a lot of pain. The problem was, I was holding on and living in error, and God will never let his people rebel in peace.

In 2 Samuel 24, David desperately wanted to conduct a census. He just would not let it go. So, he ordered a census to be taken. His rebellion brought warfare on himself and others. Some people even lost their lives because of David's rebellion. The Bible says this stirred the anger of God.

In the 10th verse, David realizes that he was wrong. He confronted his own decisions. Although he achieved restoration through repentance, his rebellion cost him and Israel dearly. They lost seventy thousand men because David would not let his desire for a census go.

We see another example in Joshua 9, where Joshua and the Israelites found themselves in a dangerous relationship with the Gibeonites. According to verse 14, they did not take counsel from the Lord and entered into a covenant that God disapproved of. Had they sought and obeyed the counsel of the Lord, they would not have ended up fighting an avoidable battle.

One of my favorite passages of scripture is 1 Tim. 4:16. Paul writes from a very fatherly and tender perspective, but in his pastoral epistles to Timothy and his pastoral epistles to Titus, he never fails to challenge them as individuals.

When Paul says, "Watch your life and doctrine closely," this is not simply doctrine as it relates to subjects, like soteriology and pneumatology and things of that nature. This is a doctrine as it relates to what we are teaching ourselves about ourselves. What things we are holding on to.

Even holding on to the manifestation of things that we should have or need to let go of is not healthy. Remember, you can't be given shame or offense or pride or anger or even disappointment. So, whenever we have these things, it's not because they were given to us. It's because we have taken them. And if we have taken them, then we can release them and let them go.

When we let go, forgive ourselves, forgive the situation, accept that it happened, but now it's over. Then we can genuinely have emotional, spiritual, and psychological freedom and healing.

Letting go is self-imposed closure. It is self-administered medicine and self-applied deliverance from the invisible chains holding us hostage, to lesser while keeping us from greater.

Again, wisdom and discernment help us identify what things we must let go of.

Some things are a given that we should let go of, like the things spoken of in the first few paragraphs of this chapter. Here they are again, just as a reminder; Pain, disappointment, offense, guilt, unforgiveness, pride, lack of confidence, haunting voices of shame, crippling relationships, covenant agreements with laziness, irresponsibility, and disfunction.

By no means is this an exhaustive list. But, it's a relatable list. Let's discuss some things categorically we should let go of.

Anything That Requires You to Live in the Past, *Let It Go.*

Forward is the direction you must live in. Isaiah 43:18 and Philippians 3:13 are two of the many scriptures that encourage us to let go of the past. Moving on is not the same as letting go.

Things only become different when you stop going backward and start going forward. Choosing this approach doesn't mean that you have no respect or appreciation for what was. It means that you respect your future enough to give it a fair and honest chance. High impact people relish in the art of consciously letting go of the past.

Old injustices and past hurt keep us stuck. They prevent us from having real joy living our best lives. The past is like a shadow that desires to cloud our future. The relationship that didn't work, the parent or relative that disappointed you, the poor decisions you made, the friend who betrayed you. These things may have really happened to you, but it's all in the past. Don't let it be

Anything That Smothers Your Authenticity, *Let It Go.*

Upon first glance, I am probably one of the most non-Pastor-looking ministers you will ever meet. I wear earrings in both ears. For seven years, I wore dreadlocks. I have tattoos on both arms. I laugh aloud. I watch cable news more than I do Christian television, I appreciate a nice glass of wine, and there are some other uncharacteristic or unconventional things about me.

Many people will have an idea of what you should be like and how you should be. For a long time, I sacrificed who I was for who others believed I should be. I tried to submit to everything people wanted to make me. Let me tell you, that was of living is garbage. It only creates misery, and you will drive yourself crazy, trying to live up to it.

This doesn't mean there is no room for improvement. It means that whenever you have to choose between authenticity and acceptance. Choose authenticity. Your tribe and your people will come to you.

It is far better to lose something or someone because of who you are than to hold on and pretend to be something or someone you are not.

Don't compromise your authenticity just to be included. The pain of rejection is stinging and challenging, but a broken heart is easier to heal than a shattered identity. Believe me, it's better just to let go of the things that tamp down your authenticity. Don't lose yourself because you're afraid to take a chance on being yourself.

The fear of failure can be a motivating factor in holding on to some things, even if the things you're holding on to are stifling your greatness, hindering your progress, and stealing your authenticity.

What I've learned from myself is that I don't have to be anybody else. Myself is good enough. – Lupita Nyong'o

Anything That Compromises Your Values and Morals, *Let It Go*

Compromise is a necessary part of life. And it's ok to compromise on things like where to eat lunch, what color car to purchase, what TV show to watch, and things of that nature. Compromise is the bedrock of relationships. Yet there are somethings we should never compromise on. Such as our values and morals. Our values and morals are the bedrock of who we are.

Our values and morals constitute our belief systems. Our belief system influences how we make decisions. It is the personal constitution we govern our lives by. It is a fixed framework that dictates how we see right and wrong, good and bad, and needs versus wants.

For sure, some people will do anything to get ahead. Anything for an opportunity. Anything to make a dollar. And anything for clout. Especially in a social media-saturated culture where likes, shares, reposts, retweets, clicks, and views have arguably been tied to popularity, credibility, and value.

In 2015, I was invited by Donald Trump to NYC and several other black Pastors to meet with him at Trump

Towers. There was drama, tension, and strong backlash from many people. At the time, Trump was campaigning to secure the Republican nomination. Several sound bites and video clips of him saying and doing things that no other Presidential candidate in history has been known to say or do were already widely circulated.

I remember arriving at Trump Towers that November, just a few days after Thanksgiving to a throng of reporters. Stepping out of the yellow taxi, I knew this was going to be an interesting day.

The Trump campaign billed the meeting as "100 black pastors endorse Trump campaign." Those were not the circumstances under which the invitation was extended. We were told that he simply wanted an opportunity to meet with black Pastors to talk about his platform and campaign.

The meeting lasted for about 2 hours.

At the end of the meeting, we were extended an opportunity to meet with Michael Cohen in a back-conference room to discuss further how supporting the Trump campaign could benefit our churches and us. However, I was curious about exactly what that might entail. In good conscience, I knew that there were very few circumstances under which I was willing even to consider supporting him.

Although I went into the meeting reasonably open-minded, the meeting solidly solidified what I had been thinking about him. I decided to skip the back room, take the elevator down to the lobby, and hail a taxi, which is precisely what I did.

The next few days and weeks were even more interesting. One of my peers who attended the meeting called me. We discussed some of the things they were offered and promised in exchange for supporting the campaign. Encouraging me to reconsider and retract the comments I made to the news outlets and media so I could get in on some of the opportunities they had been offered. I could easily see how the situation could be beneficial. And it was admittedly very appealing. For me, it was going to require me to make some concessions to values and morals.

Something I was neither willing nor prepared to do. This was an opportunity my values and morals required me to release and let go of.

Many people have suffered loss, avoidable consequences, and drama in life because they did not let go of some of the things that needed to be shuttered. Present company included.

Anything That Does Not Glorify God, *Let It Go*

The chief end of man is to glorify God. If we are holding on to things that do not promote the glory of God, we have to *let it go*. If it doesn't glorify God, then it's only glorifying Satan. The opposite of light is darkness; the opposite of good is evil; the opposite of God is Satan. If it doesn't glorify God, you have to *let it go*, not just things that people can see.

Some of the things we hold on to are things that nobody sees but God. Only God sees our covetousness. Only God sees the jealousy in our hearts. Only He sees the struggle with pride we have. Only God sees the obstinance and the stubbornness, and the other things that don't glorify him.

We must let it go because whatever we plug into, we ultimately draw from, and whatever I'm drawing from, I'm providing access to my life and spirit. Mystics may say that you're connecting with negative energy. Christians would say we are connecting to principalities. So, depending on what side of the faith spectrum you stand on, the thing that we share in common is refusing to hold on to negative things that don't edify.

The Art of Letting Go

Let's start at the top. First, letting go requires us to have mental courage. In my case, I desperately needed to decide that I was not going to permit the public shame, chaos, lies, or truths shared in confidence then later told define or control me.

Whenever we allow our minds to meander down dark paths, we set ourselves up and create space for mental and emotional negativity. Thinking critically about what we are thinking and responding to enables us to not latch on to thoughts and situations rooted in lie-based thinking.

Move down just a few inches to your eyes. Getting good at letting go requires your eyes. Look around and see what holding on is doing to your life. Can you see yourself thriving under these conditions in the next year? Do you see the impact holding onto and not letting go of these things is having on your goals, purpose, and responsibilities?

This was hard for me. Because in every situation, I had to evaluate things like staff members that could no longer positively contribute to the team. I had to evaluate affiliations that were sucking my energy and resources. I had to evaluate the mindless projects I had committed to. It becomes easier for us to know what we need to let go of once we start listening to what our eyes are showing us.

Swing back to your ears. Listen in the Spirit and take heed to the things you're being called to release. And how you're being called to handle things.

My situation was not entirely unique. Many people have endured similar circumstances, including politicians, business owners, athletes, other Pastors, etc. I needed to hear from people who had endured public shame and faced personal setbacks and came out victorious. More importantly, I needed to listen to what God had to say. What was His counsel to me? His counsel was straightforward, "Be still. I got this."

From that point on, I was able to drown out all of the background noise and let the process run its course. When people left the church, I had peace about letting them go because of what I had heard God say. When people stopped taking my calls and responding to my text messages, I let them be and stood on what I heard the Holy Spirit say. When it became clear that I was not welcome in certain circles, I let those connections go and rested in what I heard, "Be still. I got this."

Letting go of those things and then going back after some of them would have been like having a tumor cut out of your body and then arguing with the doctor why you can't live without it.

Next, let's move to your mouth. The ability to verbalize letting go is essential. Life and death are in your words. Verbalizing gives you your power back. "I don't have to keep this up. I don't have to stay here. I don't have to do this. I don't have to hold on to this person. I don't have to keep working here. I don't have to be a part of this. I will be ok." These statements disrupt what has been spoken over you and replaces it with the self-affirmation needed to make the bold move of bringing something to an end. You must speak over yourself. If other people's words control you, then everyone controls you.

Head, ears, mouth. Now, let's deal with getting your heart comfortable with letting certain things go.

It takes a lot of humility to accept an apology that you never actually received, and it takes deep emotional capacity to forgive people who are not even remotely sorry for what they did, especially when they think they are doing the work of God by trying to destroy you. It also takes a lot of strength to permit yourself to stop following your heart. Your heart is deceitful and wicked, according to Jeremiah 17:9. Just think about all the times your heart has tricked you.

Letting things go means we also have to bury or cremate the emotional impact certain things have had on our hearts. Forgiving yourself is just as important in letting go as forgiving others.

Now we come to the final step (pun intended) in this sensory exercise. Once you discern that you need to let go of something, walk away and don't look back. Is it easy? No! Is it possible? Yes!

Letting go makes our lives so much better, even though letting go can be intimidating because it pushes us into the unknown. But you simply must permit yourself to be intentional about trusting the process, doing the work involved, handling your business. And let it go.

Chapter Nine: Living by Faith

"Do not throw away your confidence; it will be richly rewarded." Hebrews 10:35 NIV

Faith is a tool, a weapon, and a resource. It's not just a collection of thoughts or ideas; it's what anchors our lives. It's a foundation of strength to stand upon and a swell of support to draw from. Every day and in every situation of life, we are demonstrating faith in one way or another. Everyone lives by faith. It's impossible to function in life without faith. The question is what we are putting our faith in and what are we building

Everyone lives by faith. Every day we put our trust and confidence in all sorts of things and people. When we fly on an airplane, we have confidence that the cockpit people know how to fly and land a plane. When we visit a physician, we have confidence that they are trained, licensed, and current on medicine's best practices. When we eat in a restaurant, we are demonstrating our confidence that the folks in the kitchen are washing their hands, wearing hairnets, and not dropping food on the floor.

Wherever we place our confidence, we are demonstrating faith. Faith, in its most base level definition, is confidence. It takes confidence to get through life. It takes confidence to bounce back. It takes confidence to overcome, endure hardship, defy odds, keep a family together, and complete a project. Confidence is required.

> *Have faith in who you are. Believe that you will recover, and it will truly happen. And don't judge yourself too harshly. Some things are meant to be, and you had to fall so that later you may rise and become what you are truly meant to be.*
> —*Joseph Delaney*

When we think about faith, we should think in terms of faith, not only being the system of spiritual or religious beliefs that we ascribe to, we must also think of faith as confidence. Confidence in God *and* confidence in who we are in God. Confidence that our God with keen omniscience has not only taken into account everything that would ever happen in your life but also, He has built you to be an overcomer.

Resting yourself on to this truth will serve you well no matter what comes your way. Keep the faith, maintain your confidence that, in the end, you will be ok. And if you're not ok now, then the end has not yet come.

Mustard Seed Faith

I learned something very interesting about mustard seeds years ago while visiting the Holy Land. I came to understand that there are different varieties of mustard seeds. The mustard seed referred to in Matthew 13:31-32 is the black (or nigiris) mustard seed.

Taking the time to understand the characteristics of the black mustard seed gives us a unique revelation on the qualities of resilience and determination that are aspects of faith. And appreciate why the mustard seed is used as a metaphor for faith. The Black or nigiris mustard seed has a reputation for its pungent, spicy aroma and flavor. In other words, it's a more potent variety of the mustard seed family.

The nigiris mustard seed has a quality of resilience that is unmatched. It will grow and thrive in nearly any kind of soil condition. It will grow and thrive under direct sunlight or in the shade. It is also very invasive. It will spread and take off large swaths of land if it is not tamed.

Sometimes we can have so much dirt piled on us that we temporarily or even permanently lose our confidence in God and ourselves.

In scripture, the word faith is used as a noun (pistis). An adjective (pistos) and as a verb (pisteuo).

As a noun, faith refers to what is believed and often points to a body of teaching (Acts 14:22 ; 16:5 ; Romans 14:22 ; Gal 1:23).

As an adjective, faith describes someone trustworthy, reliable, or faithful (Matt 25:23 ; Col 1:7 ; Heb 3:5 ; 1 Cor 1:9 ; Heb 10:23)

As a verb, faith is the act of believing and means to trust, believe in, and have confidence in something or someone (John 3:15; 16 ; 18 ; 36 ; 20:31).

The one thing the black mustard seed needs to grow is to be planted. As long as it is planted, it will grow. Do you have the seed of confidence planted in you? Of course, you do!

There are many schools of thought about why we should not believe in or have confidence in ourselves. Some say it is prideful to have confidence in yourself. However, to have confidence in God is to have confidence in yourself because of God. After all, you have been made in His image and likeness. He lives in you. And the same power that raised Jesus from the dead dwells in us.

Therefore, if I don't have confidence in myself, then it's actually because I don't have confidence in God. It is in Him that we live and move and have our being (Acts 17:28).

The most critical thing when things seem to be falling apart is to find faith in yourself. People who neglect to find confidence and faith in themselves don't always come through so well. Sometimes they don't come through at all. When your money, status, education, or affiliations can't pick you up, your faith in God and in what God has put in you is what will bring you to your feet after you have been knocked to your knees.

Case Study on Confidence

He was not supposed to be there. He should have been in the field. Instead, he was in the winepress grinding wheat. His loss of confidence had driven him there. So, when the angel of the Lord shows up to encourage and mobilize him, his response is somewhat cynical.

The angel opens up the conversation by saying to Gideon, you are a mighty man of courage, and the Lord is with you.

Gideon was in a crisis of confidence. He tried to reason with the angel that what he was saying simply could not be true. God was not with him, and he was not mighty. Gideon could not accept the words of the angel because his feelings had hijacked his thought processes. He needed his confidence restored. He would not confidently see himself as he should without first seeing his God as he should.

However, we feel about ourselves is, in some way, a reflection of how we think about God.

Living by Faith

What does it mean to live by faith, and how do we do it?

It starts with believing you are who God says you are. Confidence is established and or stolen through identity.

Look in the mirror and remind yourself who made you! The God that made ax heads float pulled spring out of winter, turned caterpillars into butterflies, provided bread in the wilderness, made dead men live, deaf men hear, mute men speak, blind men see, crazy men sane, saved wicked men, used challenged men, called questionable men and loves every man; is the same God that made you and is on your side!

Not only did He make you, but He made you capable of abounding, He made you resilient, and he made you with the capacity to defy odds, overcome setbacks, shatter glass ceilings, run through troops, and leap over walls (Psalm 18:29).

You may have to write words of affirmation, scriptures, and positive statements on your mirror. You might have to create voice notes for yourself and listen to them. Whatever you have to do to remind yourself of the origins of your creation, *do it*. You have been fearfully and wonderfully made. Be confident in this.

Pressure works overtime to produce amnesia and make you forget who you belong to. Sit in a corner and talk to yourself if you have to, but get to work on building up your faith.

Having faith in God is indeed the precursor to every good thing. Scripture tells us this in Hebrews 11:6. Having faith in God is a correct approach to living, but if we only have faith in God, without having faith in who we are to, before and in God, we lack a comprehensive approach to living by faith. A comprehensive approach to living by faith must include confidence in who we are in God. Without this type of faith, we sell ourselves short, deny ourselves possibilities and opportunities, and create portals of access to low self-esteem and give the warfare against our confidence more ground.

A lack of faith in who we are in God means that when difficulty and challenges arrive or we experience personal setbacks and make mistakes, or life gets hard, we will allow ourselves to be covered in a shroud of shame. Instead of having the confidence that God has the power to redeem all things.

Living by faith means we operate in confidence. Living by faith means we agree about who God says we are. Living by faith means we accept the righteousness afforded to us through the resurrection of Jesus Christ. Living by faith means we accept God's word as truth. Living by faith means we persevere, endure, repent, and hold fast to the substance of things hoped for. Living by faith means we give God the final word in all matters.

If, like Gideon, God sends a messenger to you in your hard place during a time of weakness and announces that you are strong. Accept the word being spoken over you.

Confidence Shakers

Gideon, Moses, Abraham, even Jesus all experienced their confidence being shaken. You and I will experience similar moments. Many things in life can and will test the veracity of our confidence. The question is, how do we seize upon these things to help make us better and build more confidence? And what are some of the things that scheme against our confidence?

Guilt can shake our confidence. When we have done something(s) in life that we are not proud of, guilt creates a negative self-image in our minds. This negative self-image magnifies our poor decision(s) and minimizes God's grace. When God created, designed, and called us, He factored our stupidity in. He's not surprised by our stupidity and blunders or the things that we sometimes do intentionally or unintentionally to sabotage our lives.

Rejection can shake our confidence. No one likes rejection. And few things impact our soul like rejection. Rather it is a job that we didn't get. A project that didn't get accepted. A relationship interest that falls through or a friend that stops responding to your messages. Rejection can be brutal, and if you let it, rejection will diminish your confidence. Remember that you will always have acceptance and an audience with the people that you need. God will see to it. And you will always excel in the areas that are vital to your success.

Toxic relationships can shake our confidence. The way others treat us leaves an impression on our souls. Negative relational interaction can rattle us and make us question our self-worth. No matter how hard we try to avoid them, toxic people will sometimes make their way into our orbit even if they do not appear to be toxic at the outset.

No one can make you feel inferior without your consent. - Eleanor Roosevelt

Comparison can shake our confidence. Someone once said, "comparison is the thief of joy." Measuring our lives by others' lives sometimes causes us to have a dismal view of ourselves or limited appreciation of our lives. This can make us feel like we are lacking or lagging behind and disturb our confidence. Perpetually comparing ourselves to others and thinking that we are not good enough has a way of scheming against our confidence.

One of the areas that the enemy traffics in is low self-esteem, shallow confidence, or lack of confidence. Comparison is a highway to your self-esteem. Many people don't experience success in life simply because they're not confident that they can succeed.

Faith Sees Things Differently

2 Peter 1:5 tells us that we must add to our faith. One of the things that we are to add to our faith is knowledge.

Adding knowledge to our faith then helps us to add perseverance to our faith.

Think with me for a moment. What if we began to see faith not only as a shelter over us but also as a foundation beneath us. Adding knowledge then is like putting up walls, and adding perseverance is like adding insulation to the walls. That same portion of scripture says that these things will, wait for it.... they will keep us from being ineffective and unproductive.

The surer you are about who you are, the more successful you will be at overcoming the internal impact of adversity.

There is absolutely nothing and no-one that has the right to take you out of the game of life. You have to know that nothing is that powerful. No one has that kind of weight, and nothing has that kind of dominion to expel you from the game. It can only happen if you lack the confidence needed to guide you through the terrain of life. Take confidence in knowing. *Greater is He that is in you than He that is in the world.*

Sometimes, you will need to regroup and recreate yourself, and you can! (Keep reading!)

In Genesis 39, Joseph is confronted with an opportunity. However, the opportunity would cause him to do something that would violate his values and morals. I believe that Joseph took the stand for righteousness because he did not want to violate God's laws and his own conscience and because he had an abundance of faith in who he was in God.

Through Joseph's dreams, he came to understand that God had a big plan for his life. He was going to rule over his brothers and even his father one day. Joseph was confident. He believed that having an affair with Potiphar's wife was not how God would bring his dream to pass. God was not going to require him to accept her proposition in order to see the manifestation of his dreams come to pass.

Faith is confident that whenever you try to make a blessing, you will end up missing a blessing.

Joseph not only ends up going to jail for something he did not do. He was also forgotten about for two years by Pharaoh's butler. Here he is perhaps feeling like a fool and a failure. Maybe even feeling like God had played him.

But remember, faith sees things differently.

Faith sees delay as more time to prepare. Faith sees grief as an opportunity to become more compassionate. Faith sees adversity as a call to endure, and faith sees setbacks as an opportunity to start over. But not from scratch from experience. Because faith is fully persuaded that for every situation there is a grace to match it (2 Cor 9:8)

Faith even optimistically sees failure. Listen, take it from me. Take it from anyone of notoriety for that matter. You will fail. And sometimes, you will fail miserably, publicly, and repeatedly. Some of your failures will be minutia. And some of your failures will be grand. But none of your failures are final. Be confident about this.

So, don't jump off the bridge. Don't take those pills. Don't put that gun to your head and pull the trigger. Have faith in yourself. Be confident. You deserve life. You deserve to live to attend your victory party when your battle, judgment, or warfare comes to an end. You deserve to live to sit at the table that is prepared for you in the presence of your enemies.

I have endured many ups and downs, many ins and outs, and many tests and trials; and have suffered from things that I was putting myself through. I'm thankful that I never totally lost confidence in where I stand with God. My faith just would not let me see it any other way.

I never felt like I couldn't speak for God again or lead God's people again. Did I need a time out? Yes. Did I need to sit on the bench for a minute? Yes. Did I need to call some things to order about myself? Yes.

All the while, I was confident that I could rise above anything that occurred in my life because God is omniscient and all-knowing, and He knew every challenge that I would ever face. And His tender mercy and loving-kindness are over all of His works (Psalm 145:9)

He knew that I would never have my father's last name. He knew that I would be born to a teenage mom. He knew that I would be raised in public housing. He knew that during the majority of my childhood, my parents would be battling addiction. He knew all of these things.

He knew every bad mistake and every wrong decision that I would make, and yet and still He decided to put something in me that he could get glory out of and that others could benefit from. Having confidence and faith in what God has put in me has helped me keep my feet on the ground. It's the kind of determination and resilience the black mustard seed embodies.

Faith Seizes the Moment

Back to Gen. 39. After Joseph was accused of sexual harassment by Potiphar's wife, he was thrown in prison. There, he met the butler and baker and used his dream interpretation gift to interpret their dreams. He told the baker he would be beheaded, and he told the butler he would get his job back. It happened just as Joseph said it would. The butler was released, but Joseph ended up serving two more years in prison. However, he went on to become the second in command of Pharaoh's kingdom.

An opportunity arose for Joseph to interpret Pharaoh's dream. Although Joseph was forgotten about for two years, and the butler did not immediately honor Joseph's request to be remembered. When the opportunity came for Joseph to do what he does, he did it.

Don't let delay, bitterness, lack of support, or fear of failure keep you from seizing an opportunity to rebound and reestablish your life—just one demonstration of confidence. One manifestation of faith can change in one day what has lasted for years. You must seize the moment and trust God for the consequences.

I fully believe that Joseph had faith in God and confidence in himself even after all those years in waiting.

The moment you start confidently attacking the things designed to shake your faith, commit to seeing things differently, decide to be resilient and persistent like the black mustard seed, seize opportunities and grow in the knowledge of your identity in God. This is the precise moment your thoughts will begin to shift higher.

Public Shame

I find it interesting that it doesn't appear in scripture that Joseph ever got his name cleared. He was never vindicated or exonerated from the scandal with Potiphar's, and the records of his situation were never sealed. Potiphar's wife never came forward and gave any public speech declaring that she was wrong and had lied. Joseph had to live with the stigma for the rest of his life. If his culture was anything like ours, there was always someone ready to condemn him for what they thought he might have done, regardless of the truth. Or even what he perhaps did do but is covered by God's grace.

Commit to crushing whatever personal beliefs you have about yourself that are holding you back. Commit to confidence.

Think about all of the things you've crushed in the past— the first day of kindergarten, your first easter or Christmas speech, etc. You were being trained to have faith in and believe in yourself. Now keep building on that early confidence. Great things are in store for you.

Chapter Ten: Double Standards are a Necessary Reality

"…but the one who did not know it and did things worthy of a beating will receive only a few [lashes]. From everyone to whom much has been given, much will be required; and to whom they entrusted much, of him they will ask all the more."
Luke 12:48

Double standards have gotten a bad rap, in my opinion. Sure, we say we want a world where everyone is treated the same. The reality is you and I both know this simply is not plausible. Neither was it ever intended to be that way. Based on Luke 12:48.

There are a different set of expectations and principles that you must govern yourself by, based on your status, the influence you wield, and your responsibility. This is a positive thing, and the universe is better because some double standards exist. The question then becomes, how should we fold such truth into the constitution of our daily decisions? It begins with genuinely valuing and acknowledging who you are, your influence, and your responsibilities.

If a young lady mismanages her personal finances, she will have to deal with the consequences and impact on her household. However, if the city manager or mayor of a city mismanages the city budget, will the impact and consequences be the same? No. There is much more at stake simply because many more people are affected. And they are affected in different ways.

The city manager or mayor is accountable to hundreds of thousands of people. There are pensions and public services at risk, not to mention public safety. Consider this, if an Uber driver oversleeps and misses picking up three scheduled passengers, a few people will be inconvenienced and have to secure alternative transportation. However, if an airline pilot oversleeps, it could disrupt hundreds of passengers' travel plans and take the airline a few days to get everyone where they need to be.

The truth is that double standards exist everywhere.

I have learned the hard way you will be judged based on your profession, position, and status in life. You will also be judged in line with your purpose and the corresponding expectations, and sometimes, you may be judged according to your potential.

Is it fair? Perhaps not. Is it life? Absolutely, it is.

Most of our lack of appreciation regarding double standards is, well, wrong. However, they are not going away, so we must learn to navigate them.

I could not fathom why some people were so up in arms about some of the things they heard about me for the life of me. When I began to consider my influence, calling, position(s), potential, and purpose, then it dawned on me why some people were so profoundly affected.

According to Eph 5, some things should not even be named among or associated with the people of God. I failed to take this to heart and keep that imperative before me. I lost sight of the fact that I had been blessed with the grace to live according to a different standard.

Grace not only covers our sins. Grace gives us the power to live sensible, upright, and noble lives, according to Titus 2:12.

I was supposed to avoid even the appearance of evil, and I had not. Through my carelessness, I had set myself up to be a sitting duck. I forgot. Purity and humility provide us with security.

I needed an awakening about my influence. No matter how common or normal I perceived myself to be, the reality was and is; I'm a man of God. And, by virtue of the standard and expectation that the Lord has of me, and that people have of me, I must live a little above the bar.

A double standard is when one rule or code of conduct applies to one person or group of people but not another, holding one set of standards for one person, one set of standards for another.

Equal but Not the Same

In life, we sometimes argue against the justice of double standards. However, double standards keep the world's equilibrium relatively balanced because people who have more influence and resources are required to be more circumspect about how they use these assets. They are expected to steward their resources and opportunities in ways that benefit others.

The challenge for me was avoiding the danger of being "conveniently" regular. It's easy for us to claim, out of convenience, that "I'm just a this" or "I'm just a that," but when it serves our purposes, we put the other hat on, i.e., "Well, I'm such and such, and I'm so and so." I have had to settle in my spirit that by virtue of who I am and whose I am, I will always be criticized just a little sharper and judged just a little more severely. Simultaneously, if I manage my influence correctly, I will be honored perhaps with a little more honor and deferred to with a little more deference.

Imagine if the teacher and the student-operated from the same stratum, or the parent and the teacher were on the same stratum. These various demarcations in stratums have been built into our cultures and life structure to ensure harmony and order.

Double standards in this context promote harmony and order. Harmony and order are necessary.

Double standards are different from the western culture *caste system*. We're not talking about being judged and separated based on skin color skin or gender. We're simply and strictly talking about how our influence, calling, resources, purpose, and potential set us apart and create the lens through which we will be scrutinized. These things determine the level of accountability and scrutiny you have to be willing to subject yourself to.

If you are not willing to be subjected to double standards, then do nothing, say nothing, have nothing, achieve nothing, build nothing, and dream of nothing. Because the moment you venture into any of these things, you consent to different standards and expectations. You set yourself apart. You will no longer be seen or even viewed in the same way as others.

Drawing the Line

For sure, some double standards are downright evil and unjust. And they need to be confronted.

June 17, 2015, Dylan Roof walked into the Emmanuel African Methodist Episcopal Church in Charleston, SC, and killed nine people. When he was apprehended by the police, they put a bulletproof vest on him and bought him, Burger King.

On August 23, 2020, Jacob Blake broke up a fight between unrelated parties, and he was subsequently shot multiples times in the back by the Kenosha, WI, police.

One man was white (Roof); the other was black (Blake). One was shown compassion (Roof); the other was left fighting for his life (Blake). This is an example of wicked double standards.

Other examples of wicked double standards exist in health care inequality, public education, equal pay for the same work, gender bias, and law enforcement officers' ability to claim immunity when they violate citizens' rights.

Know Where You Stand

My pastor helped me gain a renewed understanding of the unavoidable reality of double standards. He publicly chastised and rebuked me through an open letter. It was printed in a national newspaper, circulated online, and shared on the blogger circuit.

As if that were not enough, he then insisted that I apologize to my spiritual brothers and sisters in our covenant family. I thought, "Wow, really?! this is not fair at all!" and within myself, I immediately began to contemplate the situations and entanglements of others that do not net the reaction I was getting. As painful as it felt at the time, I accepted his open rebuke, and I honored his insistence that I apologize to our covenant family. For sure, I felt like he was singling me out and picking on me.

However, in taking time to quiet my spirit and listen to him minister when he later visited my church, I realized something. Absolutely, he was treating me differently than others. And it wasn't merely because of what happened, but it was because of who it was that it happened to me. His response to my situation was precisely because it was me. Is that a double standard? Maybe? Was it necessary? Absolutely.

I had not yet fully come to know my place of standing. He would have been less than my spiritual father and pastor had he acquiesced to my feelings and emotions and not dealt with the matter as pointedly and even as publicly as he did.

The way chastisement and judgment come into our lives is a result of this concept of double standards, which isn't always a bad thing. How many times did your parents chastise you while letting one of your siblings' slide because they knew, "you know better."?

> *There are moments throughout life where*
> *we feel discomfort and pain of being*
> *judged by another. Being graceful in light*
> *of this will help you to recover quickly.*
> *- Author Unknown*

I have learned, when people expect more of you, require more of you and hold you to a higher standard than the standard they hold others to. They are paying you a huge compliment.

You should throw away the idea that all double standards somehow or another create harm. Instead, focus on the value that double standards can potentially add to your life, how they can make you better. And keep you grounded and accountable. Reminding you that to much given, much is required.

Just Accept It

Foolish decisions are sometimes made in the crucible of low standards. Suppose you do not value certain parts of your life, respect who you are, and have a good understanding of your purpose and influence. In that case, you are creating a powder keg for disappointment, personal setbacks, and perhaps even public shame.

We all need standards. Even if they require a little more of us, stretch us a little further, and make us dig a little deeper.

In some contexts, double standards have gotten a bad rap. One of my strengths, or perhaps weaknesses, is, I have never really cared what people thought about me. The same is true today. Only people who I am close to understand this about my personality. I don't spend an exorbitant amount of time trying to manage or evaluate other people's opinions or perceptions of me. I choose not to try to correct any negative thoughts anyone might have of me. Admittedly it's a very counterintuitive approach to living.

I tend to say matter-of-factly how I feel about things and live to the beat of my own drum (within reason). This has been interpreted at times as arrogance, pride, and, sometimes, narcissism. However, I have learned that a lack of concern for people's thoughts about us does not exempt us from their criticism, ridicule, or judgment, nor should it. Whether we accept it or not, everyone has an impression in their mind about how we should be.

Accepting double standards as a necessary reality is not about turning lemons into lemonade. It's about learning to digest lemons.

The bank teller who steals money from the bank will be judged, but not as severely as the CFO who pillages the company's pension fund. The police officer who shoots and kills an unarmed man will be judged differently from the store owner who shoots and kills an unarmed robber. These are called double standards, and I have learned that they are necessary. And in some ways, even biblical.

When Israel rebelled, they got stuck in a wilderness for 40 years. When Moses rebelled, it cost him the promised land.

In the context, I am referring to them in, double standards establish expectations and promote accountability. They discourage the abuse of power and influence and encourage us to be circumspect. They challenge us to be good stewards of our influence, respect our calling, honor our responsibility, and lie up to our full potential.

Chapter Eleven: Some storms are gifts from God

"And He got up and [sternly] rebuked the wind and said to the sea, "Hush, be still (muzzled)!" And the wind died down [as if it had grown weary], and there was [at once] a great calm [a perfect peacefulness]."
Mark 4:39

For nearly two years, things in my life were very, *very* chaotic. Six months into the mayhem, if anyone had asked me how I was doing, I would have lamented that I was in the worst, most unbearable season of my life. I had been lied on, betrayed, accused, videoed, recorded, set up, charged, maligned, counted out, and forced off the church property on a Sunday morning by the police. The bank tried to get me fired, and my church was under a shroud of darkness.

Some of the men and women I had walked with and served with in ministry would not return my calls or respond to my text messages. I was shunned. People I had made personal sacrifices for and considered friends ghosted me. It was not a good situation.

After about 18 months of this, my entire interpretation of the season changed. ⬛The Holy Spirit gave me an epiphany. It fell on me gently like a morning mist. Some people called it a scandal. I was learning to call it a storm. After every storm, a rainbow appears. It is God's covenant sign.

In my case, the storm was still raging, but the sun was starting to peek through the clouds, and my perspective was shifting. I began to see God redeeming the storm and turning it into a gift from God. While I do not believe that God caused it, I am confident that God used it.

> *You may encounter many defeats, but you must not be defeated. In fact, it may be necessary to encounter the defeats, so you can know who you are, what you can rise from, how you can still come out of it.*
> *— Maya Angelou*

Storms Make the Changes We Won't Make

One of the amazing things about storms is that they change things that we don't realize the need to be changed or are unwilling to change.

Sometimes we have relationships, connections, employees, affiliations, and associations we are plugged into and have become very satisfied and content with even though we know some of them have far exceeded their expiration date. A storm can be a blessing to us because it makes the changes that need to be made. And, without a little wind blowing through, we probably would never make.

I can identify with all of the above. I had sat on my hands about things I really should have been moving on. But because of familiarity and wanting to hurt anyone's feelings and a host of other superficial reasons, I was stalling.

Storms Move the Things We Can't Move

Years ago, one of my mentors and his congregation were in the early stages of building a new edifice. The renderings had been completed, the financing secured, and the site excavation and construction was soon to begin.

When the contractor went to apply for the building permits, an issue was discovered. Right slap in the middle of where the sanctuary was supposed to be, there was a tree. It was discovered that the tree was over a hundred years old. It was a rare tree and could not be cut down, uprooted, or disturbed in any way whatsoever. My mentor and his church were devastated; after all, it was just a tree, right?

The church and the contractor tried as best they could to get the city to agree to let them take the tree down. A wealthy member in the church even offered to pay to have the tree relocated. The city was having none of it! The tree was there to stay. And under no circumstances could it be disturbed.

For months the church and the city went back and forth over this tree. The contractor began to try to figure out how they could build around the tree. That created another issue and a new set of challenges. It seemed like an impossible situation. The lot was already going to be challenging enough to build on.

The church held regular prayer meetings, asking God for favor, wisdom, and direction regarding the building project. Nearly six months into the ordeal, the pastor and church were heavily leaning towards selling the lot and looking for land elsewhere. They set a church meeting to decide what they would do next.

The night before the church meeting, a major storm blew through the city. The storm took out power lines, overturned trash cans, sent debris hurling through the air, and uprooted that tree that had caused the pastor and church so much concern.

Even with the fierceness of the storm, no one expected that tree to become a casualty. A few weeks later, the church's building plans were approved by the zoning board, and the permits were issued. Today, that church building stands where the tree once stood.

Sometimes change requires a move of God. When we are up against long-standing and deeply rooted challenges, all of the will power in the world will not rescue us. But God knows how to bring down the things that need to come down.

Storms Clear the Path for New Things

Storms make decisions for us. There were many decisions to be made in my personal life that, as a leader, I honestly knew were long overdue. I was stalling. Perhaps I was intimidated by the potential backlash. Perhaps I was unprepared to have the necessary but uncomfortable conversations. Perhaps I was unaware as to how to handle certain situations. If we wait for a storm to make decisions for us, the downside to stalling is that it often takes more from us than we were prepared to lose.

Storms Expose and Enlarge Our Capacity

Some people don't know how much strength or endurance they have until a storm comes. Every storm makes you a little stronger, a little wiser, a little more compassionate and empathetic than the previous storm.

Storms Teach Us How to Process Pain, Accept Grief and Spark Creativity

In March 2020, the world came to a sudden and abrupt halt. The Coronavirus made the world immobile for months upon months. Nearly every industry had to adjust quickly. Previously planned business trips were quickly converted to a Zoom meeting. Parents of school-aged children became homeschool teachers. People turned their kitchen tables into their workspaces. Churches ministered virtually. The entire world had to discover creative solutions to the myriad of new and unprecedented challenges.

Much of the world grieved the passing of the way things used to be and how we used to move about freely. We mourned the loss of industries, the loss of jobs, and for sure, we grieved the loss of the untold number of people who died during this time. Collectively we leaned upon each other and found solace in human compassion.

But we also got very creative. The pandemic demanded creativity for sustainability. Nearly every remaining industry had to find a new way to deliver their services and their products. Families had to find creative ways to turn their homes into workspace and classrooms. Why? Because adversity nurtures our creativity.

> *...the unique life experiences often reported by highly creative individuals suggest that adversity may have played a critical role in fostering their creativity and that increased creativity could therefore constitute a manifestation of Post Traumatic Growth. - Marie Forgeard*

Storms Bring Us to Repentance

We bring problems upon ourselves when we run away from God or when we will not walk in the will of God. And sometimes, God will use a storm to humble us to repentance and draw us back to him.

Jonah experienced a literal storm when he decided he would not go where God wanted him to go, which was Nineveh. Instead, he took a boat to Tarshish. The Bible says in 1:4, the Lord hurled wind at the sea. God sent Jonah a storm.

After Jonah is thrown overboard and swallowed but not eaten by a great fish, Jonah cries out to the Lord in 2:9. In response to this, God directs the fish to vomit Jonah on to dry land.

Arguably without the storm, Jonah would not have been thrown overboard, swallowed up, cried out to God, and then vomited out. But without Jonah's rebellion, there would have been no storm. God loves us enough to stop us and correct us when we are going in a direction that is against our assignment.

Repentance not only brings us pardon from sin. It also restores us to honor with God. To repent is not simply to admit our error. To repent is to abandon our covenant agreement with error. Storms make us more vulnerable to hear from and respond to God.

Notice we don't have an official record of Jonah's words of repentance. We discern that he repented based on how the situation was resolved. And we know that Jonah was very familiar with how God responds to repentance. He was en route to Nineveh with a word of warning. But he knew that if they repented, God would have mercy on them.

Seeking public approval is not the same as repenting before the Lord. There are not enough apologies in the world to satisfy people who have already set their hearts against you. God is not like that according to 1 John 1:9

Storms reveal the true foundation of our life

Everything looks pretty until the wind blows. Everything looks solid until the rain falls. But, when the rainfalls, and the wind blows, it exposes the foundation things have been built upon. Storms blow some things out, and storms bow some things in.

When we see cities ravished by tropical storms, hurricanes, tornados, and other natural disasters, within days of these events, emergency responders and organizations like the Red Cross come in, and people pour out generosity on the survivors. That's an example of how, in life, sometimes storms are used by God. Storms can take things from you, but they can also bring something to you.

I'm writing this book because of the storm that I experienced. I'm rebuilding and restructuring my life because of the storm that I experienced. I have relationships with people I probably never would have come to know because of the storm that I experienced. I'm able to speak to things and talk about things, and minister to men and families in a way that I would never have been able to, had it not been for this storm.

In Mark 4:39, Jesus is with the Disciples in the storm. He's not standing on the shore or up in a mountain praying. He is with them. Sometimes, life can get so chaotic and twisted and painful that we forget the Lord is there wherever we are. If we're on a mountain, He's on the mountain; if we're in the valley, He's in the valley with us.

Jesus was with the Disciples in the storm. Not only that, Jesus handled the storm in His own way and in His own time. He didn't have to get up from the lower part of the ship to deal with that storm. He's the son of the God of creation. He could have laid there in His sleep and rebuked that storm.

The Disciples riled Him to get up, but He did it in His own way and timing, as is the case in our lives. When we face challenges, difficulties, storms, personal setbacks, and public shame, God always deals with it, but He always deals with it in His own way and His own timing.

Epilogue

My life is a cornucopia of ups and downs. Just like yours. We all have a back story. Behind every decision, there is a story. Before many triumphs, there is a season or two of struggle. And some lessons are learned through failure, the school of hard knocks, seasons of stupidity - Bad timing and errors in judgment.

I have tried to write this book, not as a teacher to a student, or a coach to a player. I have tried to write in a conversational tone as a friend. Someone who can identify and empathize with you. Yet, more importantly. Someone who is rooting for you in every season and circumstance of your life.

I heard someone say, "It is not what you go through. It is what you grow through." If that is the case, then we have all had many growth opportunities. And we still have many growth opportunities ahead of us. Mistakes and setbacks in life can teach us a lot and leave us with many valuable lessons, if we pay attention.

In closing, I leave you to consider these things:

1. Success is on truly success if it is your personal best
2. There is no giant leap to better. Better is the result of a lot of sometimes little but strategic steps

3. Inconsistency and lack of discipline is the greatest threat to not reaching your goals

4. Setbacks are always an opportunity for improvement

5. Haters are actually helpers. Their hate helps you narrow your focus and keep you on you A-game

6. Mental toughness is vital. You can't be weak-minded and expect to last

7. Sharing a stage with someone does not make you their equal. Get humble. Be humble and stay humble

8. Think like, talk like, and walk like you're already where you want to be

9. Stay in faith! Never give up, never turn back and never stop believing that the Holy Spirit has put something in you that will help you win

10. Bookend every day with prayer. Prayer that roots out pride, personal sin and promotes holiness

11. You can do 20% more than you think you can. You can grow 20% beyond your current capacity. You can stretch 20% further than you realize you can.